I0389878

R.A. GOAL'S WORDS FOR THE FUTURE

HS Press

R.A.GOAL'S WORDS FOR THE FUTURE

MESSAGES FROM A SPACE BEING TO THE PEOPLE OF EARTH

RYUHO OKAWA

HS PRESS

Original title: *R. A. Goal - Chikyu no Mirai o Hiraku Kotoba -*
HS Press is an imprint of IRH Press Co., Ltd.
Tokyo
ISBN 13: 978-1-943928-10-1
ISBN 10: 1-943928-10-X

The opinions of the spirit do not necessarily reflect those of Happy Science Group.
For the mechanism behind spiritual messages, see the end section.

Contents

3 Stick to Your Beliefs in This Time of Mixed Values

CHAPTER TWO

R. A. Goal's Words for the Future

Preface

The Laws have been evolving steadily. This book—the 2800th of my publications—is meant to open the path to new horizons unexplored by humanity.

A few years after the founding of Happy Science, there was a rumor in Book Town in Kanda, Tokyo, that Ryuho Okawa might truly achieve his goal of publishing a thousand books in his life. Reality surpassed the dream.

This book presents you with a message from a space being who is a certified Messiah. It means my teachings are spreading beyond the power of Earth-born gods or ethnic gods.

"R. A. Goal" is a hidden name. "R. A." stands for Ra of Ra Mu (Ra also means king) and it is the first two initials of Rient Arl Croud. In Sanskrit, *Siddhartha* means "one who has accomplished his goal" and it is Shakyamuni Buddha's birth name, so "Goal" also means Siddhartha. Therefore, the name is also a secret code for the space soul of Shakyamuni Buddha.

The revelations were given on January 1 and January 30 as the guidelines for this year.

In the Western context, R. A. Goal is like Yahweh who guided Moses and Father in Heaven who Jesus believed.

Come what may, we must live through this year powerfully, persistently, and patiently with the spirit of "With Savior."

Listen, humankind, *the time* has come.

Ryuho Okawa
Master & CEO of Happy Science Group
February 23, 2021

CHAPTER ONE

R. A. Goal's Three Messages

UFO Reading 60

Originally recorded in Japanese on January 1, 2021
in the Special Lecture Hall of Happy Science in Japan
and later translated into English.

In this chapter, the interviewer is referred to as A.

R. A. Goal

A space being from Planet Andalucia Beta in Ursa Minor. One of the commanders of the space defense force. A certified messiah. He has the ability to create an advanced civilization on a planetary scale. His current role is to protect El Cantare, who is living as Ryuho Okawa.

The Background That Led to This Spiritual Message

A UFO appeared in the early evening sky of January 1, 2021, and a spiritual reading was conducted on the spot to investigate it.

1

R. A. Goal's Three Future Predictions

R. A. Goal's UFO suddenly appears

RYUHO OKAWA
Is it in frame?

A
Yes. Please hold on.

[*About 10 seconds of silence.*]

RYUHO OKAWA
"R. A. ... Are you OK?"
It appeared suddenly. Just came out in the last hour.

A
[*Shows the screen on the video camera.*] It's showing up like this.

RYUHO OKAWA
Ah yes. OK.

A
Yes, it's in frame.

RYUHO OKAWA
The one who has appeared above Minato Ward of Tokyo. You weren't there earlier, so you must have just appeared. You are blinking repeatedly and showing some intention. It might be R. A. Goal.

Are you R. A. Goal? Are you R. A. Goal?

R. A. GOAL
Yes.

A
Thank you very much.

First message:
Coronavirus pandemic will not stop in 2021

R. A. GOAL

Happy New Year 2021. It's been a year.

A

Thank you very much for giving us guidance on various issues last year.

R. A. GOAL

They may not have been very positive predictions.

A

But it was encouraging for us to know the near future.

You've come to us today, this year, on January 1. Do you have a message for us?

R. A. GOAL

I have three messages for you. I will tell you briefly.

The first message is about the COVID-19 issue, which must be your biggest concern. Many vaccines will be developed and shot, and the pandemic may temporarily appear to stop, but the virus will overcome them and begin to spread again.

The number of infected people you are seeing at the beginning of the year is over 200,000 in Japan. The number of deaths is several thousand, maybe about 3,000. On a global scale, it is about to reach 80 or 90 million and the deaths 2 million. This is the current situation (at the time of the recording).

Oh, a plane passed above us right now.

A

It did indeed.

R. A. GOAL

Flying above us. Hahaha [*laughs*]. I guess they didn't notice us.

A

[*Laughs.*]

R. A. GOAL

Anyway, it's difficult to predict the final outcome. Although the vaccines are starting to fight the virus, it will spread in different places. Different strains will also develop, and you will find it difficult to deal with.

Judging from the current number of 80 or 90 million, hmm... well, I predict that this year, the number of infected cases will reach at least 500 million and the death toll will reach... hmm... very close to 5 million, or maybe 10 million depending on the circumstances. Whether it will stop at 500 million depends on how effective the vaccines are, but medicine will reach its limit.

Currently, one out of every hundred people is infected, but from now on, the numbers will increase exponentially. So, it's not easy to overcome the pandemic.

There is an issue of how the mutation is happening. We need to find this, too.

I think it will be quite a tough year.

Second message: The economy will continue to struggle

R. A. GOAL

Secondly, therefore, the Tokyo Olympics and Paralympics won't be held this year, either. At the end of last year, the stock prices reached the highest in 31 years in Japan, which means people are buying stock to make money because they think the worst has passed with the development of the vaccines. They expect that the economy will improve, and everything will get better. But unfortunately, it's not so simple; the struggle will last a while.

Even by the end of the year, this pandemic would not reach half the scale it would have ultimately spread. It will really test human wisdom. Endurance and wisdom will be tested. So, Japan's economy will not easily recover. The Western economy will nearly be destroyed, and so will India's economy. Only China says they are doing well now, but this is a lie and it will soon be revealed.

A
I wonder if people will finally start to doubt?

R. A. GOAL
Yes. China is fabricating their statistics based on a planned economy, but the reality is different. It's highly possible that they are suffering hyperinflation. People can't purchase things, even if they have money. They will become increasingly distrustful of digital currency. They won't be

able to buy things. China can overstate their statistics, but people won't be able to buy things. So, they will want to go overseas and buy real goods. But I'm afraid the Chinese people will be less and less welcomed by the world. This is the second point.

So, this year, the economy will continue to struggle at its lowest. As for what will happen next year, you will have to ask me at the end of this year.

A
I see.

Third message: China and Russia will likely team up, and a war might break out

R. A. GOAL
The third point is a war crisis. Having Mr. Biden as president is like having Mr. Obama continue his presidency, and this has brought out China's true colors. China and Russia will team up and begin to reach out for many things, including resources and food.

Now, since everyone is talking about "carbon-free," China will aggressively reach out to countries that produce oil or are rich in natural resources, such as natural gas and coal. If they fail to agree on economic trade, China will try to take them by force. China is especially developing offshore oil fields and underground resources one-sidedly… or I should say they are trying to forcibly take those resources without paying any money. China will intensify such moves and step up their maritime expansion activities.

The Western countries will try to counteract this, but they won't have enough mobility due to the spread of the coronavirus.

The U.S. will start to decline and regret not having reelected Mr. Trump

R. A. GOAL

Within a year, the U.S. will already start to regret not having reelected Mr. Trump.

A

Will they realize their mistake?

R. A. GOAL

I believe they will. That is, if Mr. Biden is alive at that time. He might not be alive, though.

Even if Biden passes away, unrealistic democrats or idealists will say it will be great to have Kamala Harris—a black female in her 50s—as president, but she lacks ability like Obama. She can give a good impression, but she won't be able to do anything; she won't be able to resolve any domestic issues, economic issues, or diplomatic issues. So, if she serves as president for three years, for example, the U.S. will decline in an obvious manner, as if plummeting down a waterfall.

I hope Japan will have the power to ride through these difficult times, but Mr. Suga most probably won't last another year, and the leaders that follow will all be weak. They are so weak that Japan's prime minister is likely to change every year again. There might be a coalition government, or should the opposition party take office, Japan will end up repeating the same mistakes.

So, a conflict might occur between the ones that devote themselves to China and the ones that seek their own way.

2

Japan must Aim to Take Leadership in the World

China was researching a virus that could be more effective on Westerners

A

After we received your message at the beginning of last year, we also heard from Shakyamuni Buddha and Edgar Cayce. I remember they were all talking about the worst-case scenarios in a serious tone. As I listen to you now, I get the feeling that your message is very similar to theirs and they were pretty spot on.

R. A. GOAL

I'm sorry to say this, but vaccines developed in just a year will not cure the disease. It's ineffective.

A

The death rate is higher in the West. Does this mean the virus was developed for that purpose?

R. A. GOAL
China has been researching it for over a decade. They were trying to make sure it wouldn't infect themselves. They had been researching a virus that would be less effective on the Chinese and more effective on the Westerners. It took 15 years to create such a virus.

A
I see.

R. A. GOAL
More investigations are needed on the coronavirus variants—the mutated strains. Vaccines are about to be approved in China now, but they are already saying they have successfully contained the spread. Something strange is going on.

A
It is odd.

R. A. GOAL
The truth regarding this must be revealed.

The EU members will build border walls and the EU will start to collapse

R. A. GOAL

Who will take leadership and lead the international society? This needs to be made clear. The UN no longer functions with China as one of the permanent members, and the WHO is powerless, too.

The EU also has problems. They used to advocate that the EU bloc will make it easy for people to travel freely (between EU nations), but such a bloc is meaningless now because the member nations rather want to cut off ties with other nations and isolate themselves.

A

That's true.

R. A. GOAL

In fact, this will lead to the fall of the EU.

A

Right. It's headed the opposite of what they had intended.

R. A. GOAL

Yes, not just Brexit, but the entire EU is heading toward collapse. They will be egotistical and try to shut out immigrants, just like Mr. Trump's policy to build a wall.

A

They may think they should have done the same.

R. A. GOAL

Europe will face a harsh situation and will feel like building walls. The border security will become extremely strict and they will have to strengthen controls against illegal entry. So, I think the fall of the EU will begin.

Japan should announce a policy to officially recognize Taiwan as a nation

R. A. GOAL

It's very difficult for Japan to take leadership in such a situation, but it's possible to bring together other countries that wish to follow Japan's lead and aim to build a Japan-like society. So, you should start to think about creating a modified version of the Greater East Asia Co-prosperity Sphere—in a different form.

Regarding China, they must be split internally by spreading the idea that Taiwan is on the right side. You must have a strong conviction toward destroying the Chinese Communist Party's (CCP's) monopolistic style.

A

So, we must continue to insist on that this year, too.

R. A. GOAL

Yes. Mr. Biden probably has no convictions, but Japan should work to convince the U.S. and the EU and move toward officially recognizing Taiwan as a nation. Once Japan is firmly determined, the world will be set to head in that direction. Japan may be threatened, but they must work to produce long-range and mid-range missiles which are currently being developed.

Mr. Biden can't tell what's right or wrong

R. A. GOAL

Mr. Biden really doesn't care if Japan is occupied or it becomes a battleground.

A

That's true.

R. A. GOAL

He won't live long anyway. So, he will try to make himself look good, just like Mr. Obama.

A

He's all talk.

R. A. GOAL

Yes. He'll just say something like, "Nations around the world should get along" or "Nations should cooperate with one another," but he cannot tell what's right or wrong. He's from the fifth dimension (Goodness Realm) of the spirit world, so he's a mediocre person.

A
I see.

R. A. GOAL
He's an average person, so it can't be helped. It sometimes happens in democracy. There are many similar people among the prime ministers of Japan, too.

Even so, we need to clarify where God's Will lies.

The government might limit your freedom of speech, but voice your opinion with strong conviction

R. A. GOAL
This year will still be tough. Even so, you must voice your opinion despite the difficulties you will face because the government might decide to limit freedom of speech at some point. Those who control your actions may try to control your speech as well.

A

I agree.

R. A. GOAL

They could say that your speech is baseless and only disturbs people's minds.

A

You mean, for example, because we tell people that their lives are in jeopardy?

R. A. GOAL

Right, right. The government may suppress your criticism against China, saying Japan won't be able to survive without maintaining a good relationship with China, or claiming that it's hate speech. This kind of thing could begin. However, you must stick to your beliefs.

China is obviously responsible for the coronavirus. It was China that developed the virus. I'm not sure if Xi Jinping knew the whole picture because it was being developed even before he came to power, of course. It was already in development. Then, there is also the mysterious phenomenon where the virus did not spread in China even though the vaccine wasn't available yet.

In addition, we must expose how much they (CCP) have suppressed human rights in their 70-plus years of history. It's important to bring to light the true history of China before destroying communism.

What should people do as Japan and the U.S. become more socialistic?

R. A. GOAL
More and more countries are becoming socialistic through Chinese influence. The U.S. is becoming socialized, and so is Japan.

Like the modern money theory (MMT), the trend will be to tax the rich and distribute money to the poor. The morals of the economy will be lost, the spirit of the Industrial Revolution will be lost, and economic development will stop. However, you must select what should or shouldn't remain, or weed out what developed like the bubble economy under these conditions.

A
Yes. In China, I heard that about 300,000 people in fishing villages near the Yangtze River have lost their jobs.

R. A. GOAL
They have no jobs. They have lost a way to make a living.

A
China is in a tough situation, but the government is concealing it.

R. A. GOAL
China can't reveal what's going on in their country. However, there are factions even within the Communist Party, and if they come to a point where they can no longer stand it, a revolution will occur from within.

That's why Xi Jinping is working hard to purge other politicians. Now, in his campaign to purge corruption, he's eliminating his political enemies in China, but he also has accumulated hundreds of millions of dollars overseas. So, I think the time will come when he will be taken down.

A
I see.

R. A. GOAL
I don't know if it will occur this year, though.

3
Stick to Your Beliefs in This Time of Mixed Values

There will be many bankruptcies this year, and unemployment could exceed one million

A

So, this year, too, we have to get through tough times.

R. A. GOAL

It'll be tough.

A

Does it mean we have to start the year being prepared to get through tough times?

R. A. GOAL

You should be careful not to put "Mr. Nice Guy" in high positions.

A

I see.

R. A. GOAL

Happy Science might only serve as in the saying, "Little head great wit," but it's important to say what must be said.

Some industries will be severely affected and will cause many bankruptcies. As a result, more than a million people will likely be out of work. It would be very tough to have many people living only on government subsidiaries or welfare. So, you need to think about how to create new types of companies that meet the needs of the times. You should stop depending on a big government and push forward a free market economy. The bigger the government gets, the more people will be on welfare, and that is the final stage of socialism. It's better to fix that.

The battle will not be settled this year. It will probably be tough. I think values are still mixed up. It's important to stick to your beliefs. The battle will continue.

A

Then, we have to keep the spirit of "With Savior" and live with God in our hearts.

R. A. GOAL

It's going to be a tough year. So, you need to spread the teachings and increase the number of people who believe in the Truth and spread it. And I hope that this year, you will have about 20 million believers worldwide. You don't have much power now.

A

Yes, we have to work hard.

R. A. GOAL

You know, there are a lot of airplanes flying below us.

A

There are a lot of them today.

R. A. GOAL

They're really getting in the way.

A 15-seater UFO with record-keepers and security guards

A

Lastly, I'd like to ask about your UFO.

R. A. GOAL

OK.

A

How many passengers can board your UFO today?

R. A. GOAL

Today, we can board 15.

A

Who are on your UFO?

R. A. GOAL

Well, they're in charge of various tasks, so there are... Let's see...

A

Are they all male?

R. A. GOAL

No. There are both male and female. We are here now to communicate with you. Some keep a record of it.

A

So, they help you, right?

R. A. GOAL

Yes, some are guarding the spaceship, others are taking records, and so on. We are here because we thought you'd definitely try to communicate with us on New Year's.

A

Thank you very much.

R. A. GOAL

I'd like to talk a little more, but it looks like you don't have much time today, so I made it short. Let's talk again on another day.

A
You'd come again?

R. A. GOAL
For a more detailed talk, yes. I have responsibility.

A
Thank you.

There will be bankruptcies among Japanese and American media this year

R. A. GOAL
As for Mr. Trump, the result of the election was quite unfortunate. But not many leaders can be reelected when the country has suffered nearly 20 million infections and over 300,000 deaths from the coronavirus (at the time of the recording). This is a solemn fact. At least, it's true that he couldn't get around to investigating the cause and defeating the opponent.

A

But despite the fact that the media supported Mr. Biden so much, Mr. Trump was able to get that many votes.

R. A. GOAL

Yes, more than 70 million votes.

A

I thought that displayed the greatness of America.

R. A. GOAL

Yes. People didn't believe the media, did they?

A

No, they didn't.

R. A. GOAL

It would usually be impossible to get that many votes without the support from half the media.

A

Yes, it would.

R. A. GOAL
But actually, the media didn't support him.

A
So, America is not done yet.

R. A. GOAL
In the U.S., ...this goes for Japan as well, but there will be bankruptcies of the media this year.

A
I see.

On Mr. Trump's plan to run for president in four years

A
I think Mr. Trump was the hope for the U.S., but is there any other hopeful person staying under the radar?

R. A. GOAL
Hmm, let's see...

A

Will the U.S. be done if Mr. Trump doesn't come back? Or are there other potential people besides him?

R. A. GOAL

At the moment, Mr. Trump is raising money for the next election in four years.

A

He could be aiming for that.

R. A. GOAL

He will be the same age as Biden was when he took office (in four years), so I think he's still aiming to become president.

Who would be the next generation candidate after him? Well, I think there are a few candidates.

A

You mean, there are other Light of Angels besides him?

R. A. GOAL

I'm sure there are.

A

I thought so.

R. A. GOAL

But which side was righteous...

A

It depends on humankind, doesn't it?

R. A. GOAL

Many people in the world still believe the Obama era was righteous. There are many of them in Japan, mainly the *Asahi Shimbun* newspaper and NHK. If it doesn't become clear which side was right, they (Light of Angels) won't come out.

A

I see.

R. A. GOAL

So, there need four years of... hmm... after the new U.S. administration does the opposite (of what Mr. Trump did), people might eventually understand what he was trying to do.

A

I hope so.

R. A. GOAL

If this was a war started by China, Americans really shouldn't remain like this.

A

That's true. But they still haven't realized that China waged war against them, have they?

R. A. GOAL

That's because they think based on scientism, the attitude of not believing anything without proof. But if you think about the motive behind the war, it's obvious.

So, Mr. Trump should be like Rambo and rush into the enemy. I think he will do his best as an opposing force without completely losing his political power, and apply pressure on Congress.

Anyway, I don't think the issues with China will be settled this year.

A

All right. We have to endure it and move forward steadily like a turtle.

R. A. GOAL

Yes. For more details, please ask me next time.

The UFO is oval-shaped, with the front and the back ends sticking out

A

Finally, will you tell us the shape of your UFO?

R. A. GOAL

OK. The shape of today's UFO is rather oval, with the front and the back sticking out a little. The ends of the long axis of the oval are sticking out a bit.

The top of the observatory sticks out about five meters (16-17 feet), and the lighting is... We are lighting up the

UFO to make it look like a star. Some parts are not visible on your screen.

A
OK. Thank you very much.

The investigation is underway to identify any interference of bad aliens in coronavirus variants

R. A. GOAL
You can count on me anytime. Don't think that my predictions are off the mark.

A
No, no. They are all to the point.

R. A. GOAL
We're fighting in the long term. We're now investigating whether bad aliens that are supporting China have been involved in developing the coronavirus variants. It's possible that they have been involved. That's what we're trying to find out.

If they have, it is likely that they'll release a new variant one after another.

A
You mean, the virus could've acquired something else that couldn't be acquired simply by person-to-person transmission?

R. A. GOAL
Yes, yes. That's right. We can't deny the possibility that they've received something from the aliens. We're investigating it right now.

A
I see. It's encouraging just having you here today. Thank you very much.

R. A. GOAL
We will support you this year, too. Please do your best.

A
Thank you very much.

RYUHO OKAWA

Thank you very much, Mr. R. A. Goal. [*Claps once.*]

CHAPTER TWO

R. A. Goal's Words for the Future

Originally recorded in Japanese on January 30, 2021 in the Special Lecture Hall of Happy Science in Japan and later translated into English.

In this chapter, there are a total of three interviewers from Happy Science, symbolized as A, B, and C, in the order that they first appear.

1

Asking R. A. Goal for His Words to Create a Bright Future for Earth

A spiritual backlash to our opinions

RYUHO OKAWA

On January 1 of this year (2021), I spotted (the UFO of) Mr. R. A. Goal in the night sky and talked with him. We recorded the conversation and released it for public viewing at Happy Science local branches and temples (shoja) (see Chapter 1 of this book). We were talking with him from the balcony, but because it was at night on January 1, we couldn't stay outside for too long. So, we suggested holding a more formal spiritual interview at another time and ended the conversation there.

It has been about a month since then, and some of our members may be expecting to hear the next message from him. Just recently, we published a book titled *The True Heart of Yaidron* (another space being; see p. 167), so today, we would like to hear from Mr. R. A. Goal and ask for his words to create a bright future for Earth. His message shouldn't be too different from Mr. Yaidron's, but since other space beings may feel offended if I interview just one of them, we would like to interview a few other space beings to find out if they have different opinions.

The latest issue of *The Liberty* magazine... Is it the March issue?

A

Yes, it's the March issue.

RYUHO OKAWA

There has been a big spiritual backlash against this issue of the magazine. Just this morning, (the guardian spirit of) Mr. Xi Jinping insisted on having a debate with Interviewer A (the editor-in-chief of *The Liberty*). But I tried to calm him down by telling him that we had prior appointments with other spirits. He apparently has some objections to the entire magazine.

Perhaps the backlash may be too strong, but I think it's better to inform people of other beings who also share similar opinions. I don't know the extent of your questions today, but you may ask anything that comes to mind.

Mr. Trump issued an order to disclose UFO information as his "parting gift"

RYUHO OKAWA
Last December, former U.S. President Trump ordered the U.S. intelligence agencies to disclose information about UFOs to Congress within 180 days. So, even under the Biden administration, I think the information on UFOs will be released from various U.S. intelligence agencies by the middle of this year.

We are grateful for this news because we plan to release the movie, Part II of *The Laws of the Universe* (*The Laws of the Universe–The Age of Elohim*, Executive Producer and Original Story by Ryuho Okawa; scheduled to be released in Fall of 2021) this year. Those who pursue information on such matters are often regarded as occult and labeled as a cult, so if the U.S. government discloses UFO-related information by this summer, it would make it easier for us to release various kinds of information relating to UFOs and space beings.

It is doubtful that the three UFO footages released in the past were the only information the U.S. government has; they should have several thousand to possibly over ten thousand pieces of additional information. I don't know whether they will disclose everything, but I think they will release a good amount. Mr. Trump probably suspects that some hostile nation is possibly developing weapons using the technology provided by space beings. The fact that he issued an order to disclose information shows he is sensing something. The U.S. could be faced with a surprise attack if they remain uninformed, so I think the new administration will most likely disclose some information.

When Ms. Hillary Clinton was running for president, I remember her saying she would release information on UFOs and space beings if elected. During the Clinton administration, too, it was said that Mr. Clinton would disclose it if he was reelected for his second term. But even after he was reelected, the information never came out. He probably felt it was better not to release it. After all, it must be quite dangerous to disclose this information. There may be lobby groups pressuring the U.S. government not to disclose it. Or perhaps, the government fears the risk of it being exposed to a potential enemy.

Even so, Mr. Trump issued an order to disclose the information as his "parting gift." If the U.S. government officially releases evidence, Happy Science will no longer be ridiculed or be called a cult or an occult organization merely for publishing books on space beings. So for us, it is something to be grateful for because some people criticize Happy Science as soon as I say anything about these topics.

Once the U.S. government officially admits the existence of UFOs and space beings, the Japanese government wouldn't be able to deny it completely. They will have no choice but to give orders to collect any information about UFOs and space beings.

Uncovering the truths about UFOs is also good for science

RYUHO OKAWA

Once, I watched a program on NHK (Japan's only public broadcaster) that introduced some fake visuals of UFOs. It showed four alleged images of UFOs and exposed them as fake images that could be created by computer graphics. But I found it unfair because they certainly would not use any images of what could not be recreated. In the program, Japanese actress Chiaki Kuriyama dressed up like a devil to show the images that seemed fake, and then, dressed up in an angel's outfit to expose the untruths. I published a book criticizing this program, but when it comes to matters related to UFOs, the public broadcaster takes a very skeptical attitude. So, I imagine this is generally how people in Japan feel about UFOs.

I would be happy if we could make a breakthrough on these topics this year. As a scientific attitude, too, I believe it's good for the truths to be uncovered. Uncovering the truths means the future of humankind will become clearer, so we should take on the challenge.

I can think of various potential enemies of Interviewer A, the current editor-in-chief of quite the edgy magazine *The Liberty*, but you will probably keep writing aggressively. Well, that's your job, after all. Please watch out for your safety and do your best. I'm sorry to say this, but in case you are ever assassinated by a death squad, send us your spiritual messages from the other world [*laughs*].

This may have been a bad joke, but the Chinese Embassy isn't far from here, and they may not be happy about our moves. The U.S. Embassy could also pose some danger to us, if the new staff suspect that we are their enemies in Japan. But we are just aiming to pursue the Truth. People certainly have different opinions, but these opinions can become the source of new ideas and ways of thinking. I am not trying to be judgmental and one-sidedly conclude that a certain opinion is the only truth and reject the rest. I hope people can gradually get used to our ideas and eventually accept them.

Today's topic could be similar to other spiritual messages, so I'd be happy if you could ask new questions or questions from various angles.

[*To interviewers.*] OK, let's start. Are you ready?

B
Yes.

RYUHO OKAWA
[*Closes his eyes and puts his hands in prayer.*] Space Being R. A. Goal. We talked on January 1, but there may have been more you wanted to say. You brought up three major points, but people probably have questions about other topics. There may also be something you want to say about the future of Earth. We would be grateful if you could take this opportunity to talk about such things.

[*About 5 seconds of silence.*]

2
The Outlook of the Coronavirus

When will the pandemic end?

R. A. GOAL
I am R. A. Goal.

B
Mr. R. A. Goal, thank you very much for always giving guidance to us humankind. As Master Okawa explained just now, you gave us three prophetic guidelines on January 1 of this year. But since there wasn't enough time that day, we would be grateful if you could give us some additional guidelines today.

Let me reiterate the three points you mentioned last time. The first point was on the coronavirus. You said at least 500 million people would eventually be infected and the number of deaths would possibly surpass 10 million. Your second point was on the prediction of an economic crisis, and the third was on the risk of a war.

R. A. GOAL
They are nothing but bad events.

B
Right.

R. A. GOAL
This is not good. People may regard me as an "evil god."

B
Let me first ask you about the coronavirus. We have already been given lots of information and spiritual messages about it. And the recent news reports said the number of infected people doubled from 50 million to 100 million in the last two and a half months.

R. A. GOAL
Yes, that's right.

B
You predicted that the pandemic would spread further, and you seemed to have a slightly negative opinion on vaccines in the previous interview.

R. A. GOAL

Shall we start today's discussion from there?

B

Yes, please. I would be grateful if you could give us some guidelines as foresight on the trends of this year.

R. A. GOAL

I think Prime Minister Suga aims to reduce the number of infections all at once by declaring a state of emergency and quickly and proactively providing people with the made-in-U.S.A. vaccines. He also wants to hold the Tokyo Olympic and Paralympic Games successfully to maintain his reputation and to gain momentum in redeveloping the Japanese economy as well. He must be wondering, "What's wrong with hoping for that?" I understand everyone is hoping for the same thing.

However, we view things from a higher perspective and have an idea of how Japan should be today. If people are satisfied with a future that will come as an extension of preserving the status quo, we have to warn against such way of thinking. Although bad events may seem to happen, they are an indication that some aspects of what people have thought to be right or good until now actually go against the Truth and the Will of God. We want them to realize this.

So, if people are arrogant enough to believe there is nothing human intelligence cannot solve, their arrogance must be crushed. Otherwise, they will not be able to accept any new ideas and will repel them instead. We must knock them down a peg, crush their arrogance, and make them aware that humans must start working on building a nation or a world in accordance with the Will of God or Buddha. We want every citizen to share such awareness. After all, the pandemic won't end until people realize this.

State of emergency and vaccines won't stop the virus from spreading

R. A. GOAL
We intend to do the same for China, but we don't think it's OK for Japan to remain as it is, either. We understand that people are hoping for everything to get better, especially once the state of emergency is declared and the vaccine shots are administered, and for the economy

to recover. But I'm afraid we can't allow the wrong to prosper and prevail. It is also one of our duties as advisers to correct the course of this whole planet. It would be very unfortunate if people see us as vengeful gods, but according to my predictions, I can see that a harsh future is more likely to come.

I think the Suga administration is counting on the state of emergency and the vaccines, but unfortunately, the number of coronavirus cases and the death toll will continue to increase regardless of these measures.

You may have thought that only Japan was able to successfully contain the spread of the coronavirus, but the truth was that it's arriving later in Japan than it did in the other countries. So, it will gradually spread from now on. People talk a lot about the collapse of medicine, but it's not actually the collapse of medicine; we want them to realize that medicine is not an omnipotent field of study that can replace God.

We also want people to know that many disasters occur to humanity depending on the kind of social life—society and culture—people commonly accept. It may be strange for a space being to say such a superstitious thing, but it is true. So, unfortunately, the situation won't improve much until human beings understand this. Japan will continue to struggle, much like the world is struggling now. We cannot stop the pandemic until China's lies (about the coronavirus) are revealed as well.

I don't think the entire population of Japan will die from the coronavirus, but the pandemic will not be contained so easily. Once the infections exceed a certain level, the number of infections will multiply. It is just like how lotus flowers multiply; if half of the pond is filled with lotus flowers, they will fill the whole pond the next day. In the same way, the virus does not increase little by little, or one by one; it increases exponentially. If the number of infected people hits one million in Japan, for example, it will soon increase to two million, four million, and then to eight million.

People are probably hoping for the vaccines to work—and of course I'm not saying it's completely ineffective—but the Pfizer vaccines developed in the U.S. will only be effective on about... well, probably about 30 percent of Japanese people, and the other 70 percent will still get infected. In the meantime, new strains or different variants will come into Japan and start to spread. So, while people are discussing the need for new vaccines that may take another year to develop, the side effects of the previous vaccines will start to show and cause another commotion. As a result, you will probably be overwhelmed by a sense of helplessness.

"We have the technology to eradicate the coronavirus"

R. A. GOAL

Under these circumstances, sometimes the mass media and others may ridicule your activities and say they are based on silly superstitions or nonscientific ideas. But you must continue fighting by steadily increasing the number of people who accept and support your ideas.

If, for example, one or two million Japanese become infected, people will start to subconsciously sense some kind of divine punishment at work. Even so, we have no intention of stopping the pandemic yet.

We do have the technology to eradicate the coronavirus. We have the technology, but if we use it, humans, animals, and plants may also end up getting wiped out along with the virus. So, I think it's too powerful to use on Earth.

There are some beings with a greater, god-like perspective who conclude that the world should be destroyed once and be rebuilt. Some are thinking about causing a Noah's Ark-like phenomenon.

How things turn out will depend on how much of humankind can gain this level of awareness. But if Happy Science works hard, then after some time, I think things will turn out a little better in places where Happy Science spreads than in places where it doesn't. Some signs of a bright future will probably be seen in such places.

B
Thank you.

Coronavirus variants might have come from technology provided by evil aliens

B
The coronavirus is spreading widely across the world, and it feels like the pandemic is hitting in waves. In your previous message on January 1, 2021, you mentioned you were investigating the coronavirus variants because you suspected evil aliens to be behind them. Is there a bigger movement going on that is not confined to Earth?

R. A. GOAL

You, Japanese people, have a very strong illusion of peace, so you can't imagine a nation having such evil thoughts and trying to commit evil on a national level. But in fact, there are many countries like that. They are looking for technologies that can cause greater damage to other countries—while minimizing damage to themselves—and make it seem like it happened naturally, so that they don't have to take responsibility. It's not just one country; many countries think in this way.

Sometimes, technology is provided to such countries. Some viruses can be made on Earth, but there are other types of viruses that aliens are immune to whereas earthlings are not. We know of some viruses that would jeopardize Earth if they were used. So, we are concerned about such viruses being used. But even if people demand proof in the same way the mass media often does, we can't straightforwardly provide any evidence. It's all about whether you can believe my words or not.

Now, about 25 million people have been infected with the coronavirus in the U.S., a country with a population of about 300 million, but China, a country with a population of 1.4 billion, is claiming to have less than 100,000 infected people—90,000 according to them (at the time of the spiritual message). This is hard to believe. It makes us suspect that perhaps the viruses weren't only made in laboratories on Earth. There are viruses that we space people have already overcome in the past and have developed immunity to but earthlings have not. Historically, there was an outbreak of the Plague, but we doubt whether it, too, was made on Earth.

A
Yes, it's quite suspicious.

R. A. GOAL
Right. Some countries lost two-thirds of their population, and it's doubtful that a virus made on Earth can cause such great damage. I think some viruses were brought in from elsewhere.

In those times, people were completely defenseless against forces from outer space, so they probably couldn't understand what was happening. But there are viruses that aliens can coexist with whereas earthlings cannot. And some aliens are thinking of using such viruses to help a specific people defeat their adversaries.

"Walking into" the bodies of Chinese researchers to produce viruses

A

There certainly are eyewitness accounts of aliens and UFOs from the time of the Plague.

You just said the viruses weren't necessarily developed only in the laboratories on Earth. But supposing China is using viruses produced on UFOs up in the sky, I think it's difficult to transport those viruses to Earth unless the aliens are physically present in this three-dimensional world. The Wuhan Institute of Virology in China has openly claimed it has about 1,500 types of viruses. If those include viruses from space, how did the aliens actually transport them to the lab?

R. A. GOAL

Well, it's possible to make the Chinese researchers "discover the viruses on their own" without knowing where the viruses were originally produced. They may be using a virus they happen to come across in a cave or on a certain animal while they were on a general search for some suitable viruses.

A

I think that means the researchers were receiving inspiration from aliens. We heard from Zoroaster the other day about a "walk-in," a case in which an alien consciousness takes over a human soul.

R. A. GOAL

"Walk-in." Ah, yes.

A

In the spiritual message, Zoroaster mentioned the names of two senior officials of the Chinese Communist Party. I wonder if the alien souls have "walked into" the bodies of their researchers as well.

R. A. GOAL

They can certainly do that. For example, one may receive inspiration to examine bats in a particular place and follow the inspiration only to coincidentally find something useful.

A

Oh, I see.

R. A. GOAL

It's possible to receive this kind of inspiration. There might also be inspiration that makes you wonder what would happen if you mix certain components together. Inspiration can come in different ways.

A

Right.

R. A. GOAL

Earthlings would be terrified if we space beings were to attack them from space or destroy their cities in an obvious manner. It will only establish a hostile relationship between us. So, any intervention from outer space would be better made unnoticed. This is also true in the case of an alien attack from outer space. Those aliens would probably use an unnoticeable approach; they may be thinking of expanding the power of a country they could control and annihilating the adversaries.

3
The Wisdom to End the Coronavirus Pandemic

Human wisdom will be tested in people's fight against evil aliens

A
Listening to you, I'm afraid any discussion about vaccines becomes pointless...

R. A. GOAL
That's right.

A
It will be increasingly pointless if new viruses were to be brought in one after another. Right now, Prime Minister Suga is depending on the vaccines as the only hope. He is relying so heavily on the vaccines that he would give up on everything if those vaccines did not work.

R. A. GOAL

Even the influenza vaccines would not work on a different type of flu virus, so it would be the same for the coronavirus; the vaccine would be ineffective on a variant. Now, new strains of the coronavirus are appearing every two weeks. The virus may have originally been made to mutate on its own. But ultimately, it is possible to stop all of this.

I don't know whether people will eventually realize that what is happening now is not a world war but a space war. We won't intervene in a definite manner unless certain conditions are met. If people don't understand what is good and evil on Earth, they must simply accept the current situation. There is no other choice, even if it were to look like the so-called "divine punishment" in ancient times.

Happy Science has been carrying out its activities for over 35 years since its founding. But seeing that you are still being treated unfavorably, it would be no surprise if things got much worse in Japan. Japan is also gradually losing its competitiveness on the international stage. It once had the world's second-largest economy, but now it ranks below 20th in GDP per capita. Well, nothing can be done as long as the Japanese remain unaware of the "treasure" that lies within themselves.

This is a matter of balance. We don't necessarily support the idea of eliminating every phenomenon brought on by evil aliens. Even if something were plotted by evil aliens, humanity must use their wisdom to fight against it. If you don't have enough wisdom, we can of course help you, but on the condition that you understand there are good aliens standing on the side of earthlings. If people simply believed everything got better naturally or by chance, it wouldn't be worth helping you. So, things won't improve until people realize our presence.

I'm afraid that's all we can do. We are not a hospital, so we have no intention of curing everyone who comes to us. If 80 to 90 million Japanese people believed my words, I can give a straightforward answer to overcome the current situation. But they don't believe in what I say yet, do they? My words have only spread to a very small percentage of the people. That's not enough. I'm afraid that's how we see things.

Humans must realize the limit of academic studies, medical science, and technology

A

From what you just said, I understand that faith is a prerequisite. You said people will notice that something is wrong and wonder if the pandemic is part of a divine punishment when the number of infections exceeds, for example, one million in Japan. In your previous message, you also said this year's death toll in the world will exceed one million and could even go as high as 10 million.

Do you mean the battle will continue throughout the year in terms of how much the Japanese become aware of this or how much we Happy Science can enlighten them?

R. A. GOAL

Well, Japanese people may believe they have faith in science, but it's not faith in general science because they haven't studied military science very much. Rather, their faith lies in medical science, or faith in medical schools and academic scores. Faith in such things has replaced their faith in God.

However, the truth is, there are plenty of illnesses medical science and doctors cannot explain. The world is truly full of unexplainable diseases. At Happy Science, miracles can happen and some diseases can be cured, but this is beyond comprehension for doctors. They have no ways of explaining how the diseases were cured, so they simply regard those miracles as rare exceptions. Such "faith" is a little... I want such faith in academics and other things made by humans—not by God—to fall apart once.

In the early days of Happy Science, Master Ryuho Okawa worked hard to criticize and correct the mistakes in Japanese religious studies, Buddhist studies, and other religious beliefs that are no longer applicable in the present day. He also expressed his opinions on politics. He still voices his opinions on politics and, at the same time, criticizes scientism, or the belief that science is almighty—an idea that started in the 20th century and is now a popular belief in Japan. I believe there is a need for this belief to fail.

Many scientists have also joined Happy Science. They believe in the existence of God because, otherwise, there are too many things they can't understand. This tendency is more common among top scientists. But second-rate scientists or anyone below them tend to deny God. So, I want to help you break through this wall.

You are living in an age when doctors are "taking the place of God," but I hope people understand that there is a limit to technology developed by humans. I'm watching for when the doctors will realize they can no longer save all the patients.

Rough approaches may be used to lay the groundwork for humanity to understand the space age

C

You said one of the conditions to end the coronavirus pandemic around the world is for people to realize medical science is not almighty. In other words, people must get rid of their arrogant belief that human intelligence can solve anything and, instead, start to build a nation in accordance with the Will of God or Buddha. You expressed your wish for the Japanese people and the people around the world to share in this humble attitude.

As another condition, you said space beings will allow the pandemic to continue until China's lies are revealed.

R. A. GOAL

Yes, that's right.

C

In other words, the second condition to put an end to the pandemic is for the whole world to know that China is the epicenter of the outbreak and is responsible for producing and disseminating the coronavirus.

So, is it correct to understand that the coronavirus infection that originated in China will not end unless we humans, first, become modest and abandon faith in "the almighty medical science" and, second, verify that China engineered and spread the coronavirus?

R. A. GOAL

Yes. And next up is the space age. We want to make sure people become aware that there are different types of space beings, and among them are those who give guidance to different planets.

Although you at Happy Science make animated movies about space beings, people just watch them as mere entertainment. There is still a long way to go before people believe your movies are portraying reality. Even though humans have managed to go to the Moon, Mars, or other planets, they haven't succeeded at capturing and bringing back any humanoid aliens, right? They are searching for lifeforms on other planets, but they are unaware that aliens are already among the people on Earth. They don't even know their true origin.

Master Okawa's teachings cover such a wide range, and he is trying to reveal the origin of humankind as well as the current state and the future of the universe as much as possible. It takes much time and effort to lay the groundwork for people to understand this, so we may have to take some rough approaches. This may be the only choice we can make until countries around the world get so angry that they can no longer allow the idea of the coronavirus having been born naturally. People must endure the pain until they come to feel, "It shouldn't be allowed to occur naturally."

I also intend to urge people to repent on their choice of removing the president who was trying to fight against China's evil deeds.

4

The Future of the United States under the Biden Administration

America is becoming afraid of fighting for world justice

A

Speaking of the U.S., with the birth of a new president, it seems like the 100-day rule, which was broken during the former Trump administration, has been restored...

R. A. GOAL

[*Chuckles.*]

A

People seem to be watching how things turn out and this will probably continue until the end of April. Do you have any additional comments or projections on the development and movement of the U.S. under the Biden administration?

R. A. GOAL
Well, the U.S. is a little... I wonder if they are possessed by the "ghost of poverty." Hmm, I guess they are really short on talent. I truly feel sorry for them. They have to fight under such a leader at a critical time like this... If the media couldn't see this as a problem and led the people to choose him as a leader, then it means the media has deteriorated to quite a low level.

It's very hard for me to say this, but if Mr. Biden can serve as president, you (Interviewer A) can do it, too.

C
Wow.

R. A. GOAL
Yes, I mean it. Actually, you (Interviewer A) might be much better than him. He basically has no intention of doing anything. He is just there for show.

A
In his recent spiritual message (see p. 168), too, Mr. Biden's guardian spirit said he will take action only when others

tell him to, but otherwise, he won't say anything himself. This proves he's just there for show.

R. A. GOAL

Well, that's how he is.

But this pattern was actually common in Japan, wasn't it? Especially, during the period of rapid economic growth in Japan, anyone could have served as the head of the country. But ever since the country began to experience an economic downturn, they have had problems and have been in need of a capable leader.

The U.S. will head into decline now, after experiencing a rise for more than 200 years. They actually started declining around the time of the Vietnam War. And it's true that they have become unstable as a result of the Gulf War, Iraq War, and other conflicts. This weakness has surfaced this time. I think the Americans are growing fearful—fearful of the idea that the U.S. must fight for world justice—and are trying to abandon it.

This tendency was obvious during Mr. Obama's presidency, and Mr. Biden is following in his footsteps. He is thinking it may be safer to stay away from foreign affairs, and more and more people are supporting this idea.

This is similar to the stance the Japanese are quite familiar with. Japan's stance was "to do nothing while the U.S. is protecting Japan," but if the U.S. withdraws, Japan will have to think for itself.

Although Mr. Trump pushed for "America First," his true aim was not about putting America first; he was trying to rebuild a strong America and make it a world leader. But having failed to understand his aspirations, the American people and the media, including the major internet companies—though I'm not sure if I could call them the mass media—all chose a man who just tries to avoid any trouble. A time will come for them to be held accountable. I think they will already be held accountable by the end of this year.

The need to clean up Hollywood, the source of the American-style left wing

A

I can think of two factors that can make the U.S. decline. The first is domestic issues. In the physical sense, the current coronavirus strain will mostly be replaced by new variants by the end of next month. The new variants will become dominant and the vaccines will increasingly be ineffective, causing the infection to spread further in the U.S. If this happens, there might be another debate over the necessity of lockdowns. Do you have anything to share with us about such domestic situations, including the economic situation?

R. A. GOAL

Ah... Well, it's quite embarrassing for me to bring this up because it's so ridiculous, but during the election campaign between Biden and Trump, people were arguing that wearing a mask was scientific and not wearing a mask was unscientific. They were debating on science at such a "primitive" level. They may have believed they would not get infected as long as they wore masks like the Japanese. To them, Japan may have appeared like a developed country in this regard, but even with masks, the number of infections probably will not decrease but rather increase. This will be their first defeat.

Next, the situation will appear to improve for the time being once people start getting vaccinated. But there will be side effects, and coronavirus strains stronger than the vaccines should also appear as they become resistant to the vaccines. If the cases of infection were to increase from 25 million (at the time of the recording) to 100 million in a country of 300 million people, for example, it would be horrifying. It would be similar to what happened during the Plague. Since the number could go from 100 million to 200 million in the blink of an eye, the nation will be at risk. Some Americans may think they would rather have California sink into the ocean if it means saving the country from ruin.

Well, the scope of this topic has become too large, so you may find it dubious. But we won't accept opinions just because they come from the celebrities in Hollywood. Their movies may be successful and they may be able to win the Chinese market, but we have no intention of deciding world justice based on such things. We believe Hollywood, the source of the American-style left wing, needs to be cleaned up.

The U.S. should realize China is attacking them with a coronavirus strain developed for Americans

R. A. GOAL

I think Mr. Biden intends to overcome the pandemic with masks and vaccines, but right now, the U.S. is the "most advanced country" in terms of the coronavirus infection. They are taking various measures without knowing why the infection is spreading, but if they still continue to be the "most advanced country" even after taking the same measures taken by other countries, the U.S. must realize they are being attacked with a coronavirus strain specifically developed for Americans.

They are actually under attack.

If they still don't understand they've been under attack for a year... As president, Mr. Trump himself was already saying this. But the media tried to dismiss everything he said as a lie by simply labeling him as a liar who accused the media of publishing fake news. I think they felt he was an enemy of democracy and should be removed, or wished at the bottom of their hearts that he would be banished or even sentenced to death.

It would be interesting to see when the U.S. will realize their mistakes and come to the right conclusion.

Anyway, they will soon find out the pandemic cannot be contained just by locking down, wearing masks, or getting vaccinated. This will become clear by the end of the year.

Mr. Schwarzenegger's personal greed in criticizing Mr. Trump

B
You just mentioned the situation in the U.S. Recently, Mr. Schwarzenegger's video message to the public was also covered by the news in Japan. He spoke of the activities of the Trump supporters as if they were the Nazi movement, which led me to think his view is completely opposite from the righteous view.

R. A. GOAL
Haha [*laughs*].

B

From the perspective of the heavenly world, Mr. Trump is a Light of Angel whereas Mr. Biden is an ordinary person. Despite this, there seems to be a large movement within the mass media and social media, which deal with various kinds of information around the world, to flip the values and information or to spread disinformation and brainwash people to think in the opposite way. How do you view this situation?

R. A. GOAL

Well, that's because Mr. Schwarzenegger wants to become president himself [*laughs*]. Everyone knows that he has personal greed. Greedy fish are easy to catch. He has greed.

He is an immigrant. He immigrated to the U.S. as an adult, so although he could become governor, the law needs to be revised for him to become president. That's why he curried favor with the Democrats, so he could create a movement within the majority group to pass a new law and make himself president.

He probably thinks, "If Reagan could serve as president, so can I. Reagan was only a second-rate actor, but I'm a first-rate actor. Reagan and I both served as governors, so there's no way I can't become president."

On a personal level... I'm not sure exactly, but I heard that the TV show Mr. Trump emceed or anchored ended up being canceled after Mr. Schwarzenegger took over. So, perhaps Mr. Schwarzenegger has a personal grudge against Mr. Trump.

The Chinese side and the anti-Republican people would surely take advantage of such an actor who wants to be president. They will certainly try to have him change sides and use him to gain many supporters. This is too obvious to... Well, it's disappointing, but the greedy will easily take the bait.

China will test the Biden administration through various provocations

A

Earlier, I asked you about domestic issues as one way the U.S. will decline. Another way might be through foreign affairs. The other spiritual beings we've talked to have also pointed out that some nations will take advantage of the situation if the U.S. does nothing in terms of international affairs.

I am especially concerned about China. Assuming that the U.S. becomes "static" under the Biden administration which started this year, what moves do you think China will make?

R. A. GOAL

China is moving quite fast. By the time Mr. Biden was expected to win right after the presidential election in November, they were already making their moves. For example, they were taking increasingly aggressive measures against Hong Kong.

In addition, when the WHO research team went to Wuhan for an investigation, China put them in quarantine and "detained" them for two weeks. It was as good as being warned, "We can arrest you at any time." There was no way they would find any evidence after that. This was obvious to everyone. They went to China a year after the outbreak and were tied down for another two weeks. There is no doubt China made arrangements to cover up any evidence. So, there was no way anything significant would be found.

Furthermore, there is the issue with Taiwan. China is escalating their aggression on Taiwan's territorial waters and airspace even more now. Similarly, Chinese vessels are increasingly intruding into the territorial waters around the Senkaku Islands of Japan as well.

Especially in regard to Taiwan, China can attack just by using drones, without using any missiles. If they use boats to get closer to the maritime border of Taiwan and release a drone from there, they can attack Taiwan. China has been making many drones and already has many at hand. So, by drone attack...

Of course, they are not happy to hear that Taiwan only has about 800 infected people (at the time of the recording). China can't stand Taiwan saying it has successfully contained the infection by banning entry of people from mainland China. China basically wants the infection to suddenly spread in Taiwan. For this to happen, they simply need to go closer to Taiwan at night and scatter the virus using drones. Then, the virus will suddenly begin to spread wildly. They could do such a thing.

They could also make a direct attack using drones. They have small drones that cannot be distinguished from birds and do not show up on the radar. I'm afraid China is thinking about making such moves. They are already making many daring moves around the Senkaku Islands as well.

So, I think China will pose challenges in various ways to test the ability and judgment of the Biden administration. They will probably make many such moves in the first half of this year.

Japan has to make up its mind to confront China

R. A. GOAL

Many Chinese tourists have been visiting the islands in and near Okinawa Prefecture and buying land there. The coronavirus is spreading widely again in those places as well. It's easy to bring in the virus from China. When it comes to islands around there, it's very easy.

This is a "battle of wits." The Chinese counterpart of the Japan Coast Guard has been allowed to use as many weapons as necessary to fight against foreign ships. But even so, the Japan Coast Guard still won't be able to strike them until after they are attacked. A violation of territorial waters is not a good enough reason for them to fire weapons. But eventually, there will be some clash in an obvious manner.

The Japanese often say problems should be resolved through talks, but as you can see, China is not a country you can have a proper talk with. They only talk from their perspective and always blame others. It's the same pattern every time; you can't have a proper talk with them. So, Japan has to make up its mind to confront them, otherwise things will get worse.

Well, hmm... Although Mr. Suga is not almighty, he understands Machiavellianism. He understands rule by fear, so he has some sense of resistance against that idea. But the Suga administration probably will not last for much longer. As the prime minister of Japan changes successively, many incompetent leaders with the ability of the average Japanese will stand in that position. This has already happened in the U.S.

Even if the U.S. affirms that the Japan-U.S. Security Treaty covers the Senkaku Islands, they may say it doesn't necessarily mean the U.S. has promised to do something about it. If they insist on exercising "strategic patience" and seeing how things unfold for the time being, then that's it for the Senkaku Islands. The U.S. can blame Japan and say, "Japan should have landed on the islands and built a fortress if they claim territorial rights over the Senkaku

Islands." Or they may say, "We are willing to apply the Security Treaty to the issue, but why should we protect or take back what Japan has given up?"

The U.S. has double the risk now

R. A. GOAL
The U.S. has double the risk now. The first lies in Biden being a mediocre person, or being incompetent as president.

The other risk lies in the vice president under him. Supposing that Biden falls from power, passes away, or is removed, there will be a much more fearful situation because the vice president is even more incompetent than Biden. If this vice president becomes president, Japan will face greater crises.

So, you must hope Biden will not die very easily. Something worse will happen if he does. It is terrifying to have someone who has only served as a senator for about four years to become the president of the U.S. and have access to the nuclear button. From the perspective of many experienced world leaders, it's a rare chance to deal with an easily manipulable U.S., so they will all take this opportunity to think about plotting something.

A

Could you explain what you mean by the vice president being "even more incompetent," so that the people of the world or in Japan can understand it better?

R. A. GOAL

I'm not sure whether I should say this... Well, taking an example from Japanese politics, do you remember the female leader of the Social Democratic Party of Japan? Perhaps, she is no longer the leader.

A

Yes, I do. I remember her.

R. A. GOAL

You can imagine someone like her becoming the prime minister of Japan.

A

Oh, I see.

R. A. GOAL

In that case, everything she thinks and does will be the opposite of what should be done. I think that is how it would be.

5
How should Japan Confront China's Ambitious Plans?

Taiwan is in crisis

C

Of the three prophecies on the future outlook of Earth you gave us on January 1, the third point was about the crisis of war, which is linked to what you just mentioned.

R. A. GOAL

Ah, yes.

C

You mentioned Taiwan earlier. Based on what we heard from Mr. Biden's guardian spirit the other day, the U.S. could potentially retract the arms deal with Taiwan. He said the reason for this is because he honestly thinks Taiwan will become absorbed by China anyway. He thinks Taiwan is too small a country to defeat China and should therefore just be assimilated peacefully. This was what Mr. Biden's guardian spirit said. It seems Mr. Biden himself will forsake Taiwan. Given such circumstances, what can you say about the future outlook of Taiwan?

R. A. GOAL

If China tells Mr. Biden, "Taiwan belongs to China under the 'One China' policy, so we will not allow Taiwan to seek independence and violate Beijing's sovereignty. Should Taiwan seek independence, China will not hesitate to attack it," or "The Taiwan issue is China's domestic affairs, so the U.S. has no right to interfere," he may even think China has a point because he does not fully understand whether Taiwan is truly part of "One China" or not. With such a shallow understanding, he can't take a hard-line stance. The military may express condemnation, but they won't be able to take any action if the top is indecisive.

So, Taiwan is surely in crisis.

Although Taiwan is in crisis, they have no choice but to go with Mr. Biden who only knows how to leave things up to others. He expects someone else to take a tough stand... In other words, nothing will be done unless someone else who can take responsibility dares to act. If the Secretary of State or the Secretary of Defense decides to take responsibility, they may be able to protect Taiwan, but if they are not persuasive enough, Taiwan will face a very difficult situation.

In the latter case, Taiwanese people in support of appeasement will regain power and claim that it will be safer for Taiwan to remove the hawkish president. But I think Japan's attitude will also play a big role in determining the ultimate outcome. In that sense, this year will be interesting in terms of international politics. I think there will be a lot of "prophets" and they will give contradicting opinions in many ways. So, it's going to be interesting.

Anyway, now that people have drawn a straw called Mr. Biden, nothing can be done.

Even if Guam were to be taken, Mr. Biden might not protest. He could be thinking, "Guam wasn't part of the U.S. to begin with, was it?" "There is no way such a place is America." Even if the same were to happen to Hawaii, he might think, "The U.S. may end up suffering a little damage, but it's unclear who that island actually belongs to, seeing that even Japan was trying to take it." While I don't want to use a discriminatory term, maybe this is his way of displaying "strategic dementia." I think he is just hoping he won't have to deal with such issues during his presidency.

B

As soon as Mr. Biden's victory in the election was reported, China stepped up its crackdown in Hong Kong. And I'm afraid Taiwan's President Tsai Ing-wen is in a really critical situation.

R. A. GOAL

Yes, she's definitely in a critical situation.

Keynesian economics is connected to the first Qin Emperor beneath the surface

B

On the other hand, there is no doubt that mainland China has also been severely affected by the coronavirus, even though there is little information about it.

R. A. GOAL

That's right. There's no question about that.

B

When you talked about the economic outlook in your

previous spiritual message on New Year's Day, you said China's economy is in danger due to hyperinflation. I think it is difficult to predict the course of China's economy under the next four years of the U.S. Democratic administration, but how do you foresee China's economy?

R. A. GOAL

Well, I'm not sure if I should say this from outer space.

[*Pointing to Interviewer A.*] You, too, have probably experienced this, but government officials in Japan study economics even after they have been appointed. Economics taught in postwar Japan is mostly Keynesian economics, so people in Japan mainly study the Keynesian theory.

But according to Happy Science's spiritual research, something suspicious was revealed about Keynesian economics. Surprisingly, the first Qin Emperor appeared as one of Keynes' past lives. Whereas the first Qin Emperor is in the deepest pits of hell, Keynes seems to be in the limelight today for having greatly contributed to the recovery of the postwar economy. Before that, Keynesian economics was instrumental in Hitler's plan to rebuild Germany after WWI until it gained enough economic power to fight in WWII. Japan still adopts Keynesian economics and, in a sense, China's economy is also based on Keynesian economics—Keynesian economics under communism.

The Japanese politicians are all thinking based on Keynesian economics, even to this day. They believe huge government investments create jobs, raise new industrial capital, foster industries, and expand the economy. This is their basic thinking. But if Keynesian economics is connected to the first Qin Emperor beneath the surface, then...

The first Qin Emperor certainly did something similar to Keynesian economics, such as creating the Great Wall of China and the Lingqu Canal. As a result, he made his people suffer. The people greatly suffered, but he is credited for having protected the nation from external enemies, right?

Looking at China now, it has adopted Keynesian economics and is making its people suffer, but the country has expanded to the point where it is strong enough to never allow external enemies to occupy their land, as it did over 100 years ago. In this sense, something very similar to when the Great Wall of China was built is happening. We must go as far as to expose these truths, so that a "collapse of this economic theory" will come.

A new economic theory must be formed to overcome Keynesian economics

R. A. GOAL

You are taking a modest approach and saying, "Let's go with the self-help spirit," but that approach appears quite insignificant and primitive to Keynesians. The phrase "let's go with the self-help spirit" reminds them of the statue of Sontoku Ninomiya carrying firewood on his back, which used to stand in elementary schools in Japan.

Keynesian economics, on the other hand, encourages huge investments on a national level and saves the poor. And because it aggressively promotes various projects, a nation can appear to be developing rapidly. A planned economy works very well in a nation that adopts Keynesian economics, so governments are able to implement something like a five-year plan or a ten-year plan. This kind of government appears to be superior, so Japan is strongly attracted to such an approach.

But without creating a new economic theory, you ultimately will not be able to overcome Keynesian economics. China's economy, which is like a rehash of Keynesian economics, is now leading the world using

Internet infrastructure and AI technology and is fighting to overtake America. Mr. Suga probably feels rushed to catch up because Japan seems to be left behind in those fields. But the Keynesian way of thinking needs to meet a deadlock and crumble, and a new type of economic theory needs to be formed. So, this is actually a much bigger discussion. It's much bigger.

The collapse of (the economy of) China must go as far as to demonstrate that Keynesian economics will ultimately fail no matter how much it is modified. For government officials and politicians, it is hard to give up on the theory that teaches, "Governance will succeed and people will prosper as long as the government's instructions are followed faithfully." This approach was used in the Edo period (1600 – 1868) in Japan. This was their basic way of thinking. I can understand it is hard to abandon this idea.

Will it be possible to overcome Keynesian economics? Perhaps this will take some time.

China will do anything to secure food, energy, and the nation

A

When China's Keynesian economy comes to a deadlock and the Keynesian economic theory crumbles, China's economy could face a tremendous collapse.

R. A. GOAL

Well, that's not really a big deal. After the great collapse, their economy will just return to an agriculture-based economy—the most primitive level of the economy. Their economy will simply go back to being based on agriculture and fishing.

In fact, China is making considerable maritime advancements partly because they are trying to live on fishing. Yes, that's why they are trying hard to expand their territorial waters. The Senkaku Islands themselves do not have much value, but by taking over those islands, China can take control of the waters around them. The same goes for the South China Sea. If they take over the islands there, the surrounding waters will also be theirs, which means they can secure fishing resources.

Now that the one-child policy is abolished in China, people can have more than one child. This means they need to look for sources of food. China will do anything to secure food, energy, and the country. This is their basic stance now.

China is attempting to colonize other countries

B
So, a communist country will do everything it can until it collapses in the end. Is this the kind of scenario that is awaiting in the future?

R. A. GOAL
The world still doesn't understand the pros and cons of communism even after seeing the collapse of the Soviet Union, right?

B
Right.

R. A. GOAL
China believes they can keep going if they modify communism a little. They think adopting Deng Xiaoping's theory and establishing "modified socialism" will help them succeed. And they are pretending that things are working even if they actually are not.

Military expenditures alone do not yield any positive economic effect, but if China colonizes and controls other countries, they can retrieve the money spent on their military activities. You can see this from the cases in South Mongolia, the Uyghur region, Tibet, and even in Hong Kong and Taiwan. So, China has succeeded in building colonies in those regions, in reality.

Now that the European colonial age is over, we have entered an era in which China is establishing colonies. They are trying to do the same thing the Europeans did, but 500 years later.

However, China does not understand that Hong Kong enjoyed prosperity because there was freedom. China doesn't understand freedom and democracy, so they can't understand the reason why Hong Kong was prosperous.

They believe they can own Hong Kong's prosperity once they take over the territory, but that prosperity will be lost if the people who were freely doing business there are gone. Xi Jinping cannot understand this no matter how hard he tries. He only understands the controlled economy.

China is taking advantage of the shameful aspects of American-style democracy to brainwash its people

C

Looking at history, it took about 70 years for the Soviet Union to collapse since the Russian Revolution, for example.

R. A. GOAL

Yes.

C

This year marks the 100th anniversary of the Chinese Communist Party (CCP), and some people speculate that the CCP will not last much longer considering its "structural endurance." From a historical standpoint, it seems China is in a pressing situation especially in terms of whether they can withstand the weight of these 100 years, as well as the possible economic collapse. How do you think things will unfold?

R. A. GOAL

But this time, because America exposed some very shameful aspects of American-style democracy, China took advantage of this opportunity to rapidly brainwash its people, so that they reject the idea of democratizing the country and shifting to a two-party system. China is brainwashing its people in all aspects by saying, "It's wonderful to develop in an organized way while maintaining a stable order rather than turning into a shameful nation like the U.S."

China is also trying to take over Hollywood and make the U.S. its servant. They have large ambitious plans to drag people into upholding Chinese values as superior and making the U.S. serve China.

Pro-Chinese politicians must be eliminated from Japanese politics

A

Listening to you, I sense that we are entering an age when there is an increasing need for Japan to truly rise. When you mentioned Taiwan in your previous session with us on January 1, 2021, you strongly emphasized that Japan should take more initiative and lead other countries in defending Taiwan and ensuring security in other Asian regions, especially given the presumptions about the new Biden administration.

The current Suga administration has many problems. And it's highly likely China will make some daring moves this year, as you said earlier. Last time, you said Japan should think about how to go about dealing with China or what it should do to handle those moves and to clearly express its intentions. Can you elaborate on this point?

R. A. GOAL

Well, Japanese politicians have many factional struggles that are like disputes in a village, but it's difficult for them to take action based on the macro perspective, such as initiating a strategic change in administration.

The current Liberal Democratic Party and the Constitutional Democratic Party of Japan are both quite ignorant of the kinds of crises you have been warning against. They are extremely ignorant. Neither party will admit such crises are happening unless the media acknowledge them. So, they will be very slow to act.

It's a pity that the Happiness Realization Party (HRP) is making little advancement even after 12 years from its founding. This is partly because Japan's national character is refusing to accept HRP and blocking it from gaining any seats in the diet. If the media approved of the HRP's policies and supported it, it would have grown enough to become part of the government at a much earlier stage. But the media only see it as a political movement started by a cult religion that came after the Aum Shinrikyo cult.

What actually need to be eliminated are the Komeito Party and Soka Gakkai, both of which are pro-China and were contributors to the advancement of China. I think Soka Gakkai has marked the 90th year of its founding, but even when the time has come for Soka Gakkai to end, this point is left unnoticed. There will always be pro-Chinese politicians unless the Komeito Party is eliminated.

The Komeito Party was founded by the leader of the religious group Soka Gakkai. He is a great admirer of Mao Zedong, a man who became a devil of hell after death. And this Komeito Party found its way into the ruling party and is evading criticisms by clinging to the government. Now, the Liberal Democratic Party needs this coalition with the Komeito Party to secure the majority.

Considering the root reason why Happy Science and HRP was founded, I think one of the reasons was because there was a need to eliminate Soka Gakkai and the Komeito Party. But it has been difficult to do so because of the powers they have as the preceding groups. In this sense, a "revolution" needs to occur.

In general, people tend to think religions are all based on autocratic leadership. Even if you insist this is not the case with Happy Science, people can hardly believe it. You express hard-line views in your magazine, *The Liberty*, but Master Okawa does not censor them in advance, does he? Well, your opinions probably are not wide off the mark because you study Master's teachings, but even if you write whatever you want in the articles, Master does not censor them. You are free to write anything.

Well, I guess this, too, is a big battle. A 100-year battle is quite significant—it may well determine the next 100 years.

As a nation of bushido, Japan must say what needs to be said regarding the Asian crisis

C

My question is related to Mr. A's question about how Japan should express its strong-willed intentions. Master Okawa wrote a message to the Japanese people in the afterword of *Inside the Mind of President Biden*. It reads, "O Japan, as the land of the bushido spirit (samurai spirit) you shall rise again. O before the world returns to the dark ages again, the new sun shall be made to rise by you. This is my earnest desire." Would you comment on how Japan should rise as a nation of bushido and be newly reborn as a leader to guide the world in the right direction?

R. A. GOAL

Japan has now become a "self-preserving" country that just tries to avoid problems. Master Okawa is posing the question of whether it should remain that way. To put it another way, he's sending a message that says, "In the face of the Hong Kong crisis, the Taiwan crisis, and other looming crises in Asia, Japan should be fearless of any potential damage and say what must be said as a country of bushido. If the U.S. no longer has the power to lead the world strongly, Japan must be able to convince them to cooperate."

Materialism, atheism, and scientism prevailing in Japan have actually worked to weaken Japan. But at the heart of bushido lie justice and the attitude of telling right from wrong. And even before distinguishing right from wrong, it upholds the value that surpasses life and death. Bushido is built on the idea that "A world of souls exists and those who do the right thing will return to heaven whereas those who do wrong will go to hell. So, one must accomplish the right thing even at the cost of one's life."

People used to believe humans have an eternal life and those who do the right thing in the eyes of God or Buddha shall not fear death. But now that people are denying the existence of the other world, they only view things based on a worldly sense of values. As a result, they put the highest value in leading a comfortable life without experiencing much trouble and earning some level of respect in their given fields. People must be awakened from this state.

Master Okawa is saying it is shameful for a country of bushido to have forgotten its values and to instead prioritize welcoming Chinese tourists who go on a shopping spree in Ginza or Harajuku in Tokyo. Well, I'm not sure if Mr. Suga can understand this idea to this extent, though.

6
Forces beyond the Earth's Level Are at Work

Spread the message of salvation to Buddhist, Christian, and Islamic countries

A

Leaving Mr. Suga aside, you also said harsh situations will continue throughout this year. Despite these conditions, I think we believers of Happy Science must advance our missionary work and continue to spread the Light until the world realizes God's punishment. We would appreciate it if you could give us your words on this point, especially for the Happy Science members.

R. A. GOAL

I can understand why things have taken this long. Good teachings had already been given sufficiently by around 1990, but it naturally takes 30 years for an organization to build its facilities, create a system, and nurture human resources. During that time, it may have appeared as if you were making little progress.

This is understandable. No founder of religion in the past—be it Jesus, Shakyamuni Buddha, or Moses who are revered now—was able to create a large organization in his lifetime. So, I understand that it's quite difficult to achieve this much while the founder is still alive.

Even so, Master Okawa has worked hard to come this far in one generation. It is no good if his teachings do not spread all the while the coronavirus continues to spread. His teachings must spread as fast and wide as the virus through the combined effort of the disciples and other people. But unfortunately, even if the teachings have spread, the activities lack energy, people are not taking action, and the movement has not gained momentum. This is a bit of a shame.

The disciples still lack the abilities and discernment to break through the norm of society, so Master Okawa has to fight alone. I believe the disciples must gain more abilities to be able to fight as an organization and somehow achieve 10 times greater work to dedicate to Master Okawa in the next 30 years.

The Happy Science teachings have been spreading overseas as well, but not all people who have joined Happy Science study the teachings deeply or do missionary work. There is no doubt that believers who study deeply or do missionary work are the minority. It's possible for Happy Science to spread like Christianity in 2,000 years' time, but it would have lost much of its power by then.

The current pope is from South America, so he is anti-U.S. and is virtually a communist. Because he is a communist and shares the same views with China, when he negotiates with China, he doesn't have the guts to fight to protect his churches by gaining the support of the international community. Should the U.S. and China wage war against one another, he would rather side with China. He carries a sense of dissatisfaction from being born and raised in a poor South American country. So, Christianity cannot really save people.

The fact that your teachings incorporate not only Buddhist teachings but also some Christian teachings shows that Christianity is no longer dependable. Islam is inflexible and it will require much power to spread the teachings in Islamic countries, so it may take some time to save them. But at any cost, you must spread the message of salvation to countries that were once Buddhist, the current Christian countries, and Islamic countries that are in conflict.

The disciples do not have the guts to vividly envision 10 or 100 times the current scale of activities and to actually achieve it. They have the tendency to maintain the status quo or become satisfied with making themselves look like they are making progress. This is a bit sad.

Happy Science should have more than 20 million believers worldwide

A

You just mentioned overseas missionary work. In your previous message on January 1, you told us to aim to increase the number of believers to about 20 million.

R. A. GOAL

Of course, you should.

A

You said we have to achieve that level in global missionary work.

R. A. GOAL
You certainly should.

A
That message had tremendous power.

R. A. GOAL
Looking at what you are doing, it would not be surprising if you had 20 million believers already. From the scale of your activities relative to other religious groups, you should have 20 million believers. Look at how widespread it has become. Ryuho Okawa's lectures have been aired on TV in other countries, including the U.S. Considering the activities of other religions, even 20 million is small. It would not be surprising if you had more followers. This is a modest figure.

A
Right. Considering the width, height, and depth of our teachings, we should resolve to aim for 20 million believers. Do you have any advice, especially for our believers overseas, on how we can take one or two steps forward this year, despite such difficult circumstances?

R. A. GOAL

You're in a race against the virus. You must first aim for 20 million, then 50 million, and then 100 million believers. The virus is spreading, so if your teachings don't also spread, you will have no chance of winning. So, you have to work harder.

In truth, you should have about 200 million believers in Africa, but the hands for help have not reached Africa at all.

Considering Allah has appeared to Happy Science, you can essentially count all Muslims as your believers. There shouldn't be any problem with counting them as your members, but if they threaten to assassinate you on hearing such remarks, then you cannot call them your believers. Anyhow, if your Lord protects Islamic countries as well as Christian countries, then there should be no problem counting the Muslims and Christians as your believers, not to mention Buddhists.

Well, you need to work harder. You should be aiming to achieve that level.

We intend to let at least about half of humanity survive, although many may die from the infection. But at least half of them will survive. It should not take much time for the population to double after that, so that's what we intend to do. But unless Happy Science spreads, we wouldn't be so motivated to do what we plan to do; it would be very disappointing.

Earth is becoming a "Messiah planet" of another dimension

R. A. GOAL
We have sown a lot of seeds in past civilizations as well. We created various civilizations and religions on Earth. We believe we created these things, so we don't want to be underestimated by earthlings.

Our work is not like the work of small gods of Earth in many countries or that came from other planets. Forces beyond the Earth's level are now at work. And Earth is transforming into a "Messiah planet" of another dimension, which is why we need to put in more effort.

We want to guide the revolution for the entire Earth at all costs, so that Earth can connect to other civilizations in the universe—we want Earth to be at a level where it can connect to other advanced planets. We want to achieve this within the next 30 years.

We actually are hoping to appear and speak in front of you. But this is difficult unless you spread your teachings more. It wouldn't be worth it for us to get caught and be displayed like the pandas in Ueno Zoo, so we can't make our appearance now. But if there are more believers, we definitely want to show ourselves and interact with you. We want to be able to communicate with earthlings. If possible, we want to reach that level. So, the more Happy Science believers there are, the better.

There were times when earthlings traveled to other planets

A

You just said Earth is changing into a "Messiah planet" of another dimension.

R. A. GOAL

Exactly.

A

This is new to us. Since this is a precious opportunity to ask you questions, we'd like to know, in connection to what you just said, what position Earth holds from the perspective of the universe, or how Earth looks to you and where it should head toward. We have been taught about this in many ways, but we'd love to know how you view Earth from the perspective of the universe.

R. A. GOAL

There were times in past civilizations when earthlings interacted more with beings from outer space. There are no historical records, so sadly, there is no way to confirm this. But things weren't only being introduced to Earth from other planets—there were also times when things were being introduced to space from Earth.

On a galactic level, currently, many planets are in need of help and are in conflict. This may sound like *Star Wars*, but in the future, you earthlings will have to go to other planets that are in conflict, much like the current situation between the U.S. and China, and judge what accords with justice. So, the "opposite" will happen.

A

Are you saying there were such times in the past?

R. A. GOAL

Yes, there were. But...

A

So, there were. I see.

R. A. GOAL

Yes, but there are no historical records to confirm that. You probably think earthlings were only receiving things from space beings—things like seed potatoes or corn kernels. There may have been times like that, but there were also times when earthlings set out to outer space to provide something from Earth.

Now that El Cantare is on earth, we are aiming to reach that level. If we can directly provide you with technology, you will be able to regularly travel to outer space very soon. If we are allowed to reveal the Truth, we will of course do so, but I need more people who are ready for it. Can you understand how I feel?

But the time is nearing. Although Mr. Trump was driven out of office after four years of his presidency, he accomplished what needed to be done and opened the door to the universe. Because he had a good understanding of good and evil on a global scale, he was able to understand our thoughts and ideas as well. It was unfortunate that he had to step down, but it was up to the earthlings to decide, so I can't comment on it any further. In any case, we want to do something positive, constructive, and future-oriented.

We don't know how much you can accomplish once Master Okawa leaves this world. I'm sure he will not end as a mere God of Earth and will have to take care of other planets as well. He will most likely begin working to guide other planets, just as I am now here guiding you. So, it's time for Earth to finish what it must.

A
Thank you very much.

The secret of R. A. Goal's soul

C
Mr. R. A. Goal, it seems like you and Lord El Cantare, the God of Earth, are very close. We've also been told that you had once studied with one of His brother souls. It was also a

great shock to hear that Earth has such a history we should be proud of. Have you had a deep connection with Lord El Cantare since ancient times?

R. A. GOAL

It will all be revealed at the very end, so I cannot disclose everything at this moment. But for now, you can assume I am part of the space soul of Shakyamuni Buddha. So yes, I am connected to El Cantare.

C

A space soul? Master taught us that some parts of our souls have roots in the universe. Is that what you are referring to?

R. A. GOAL

Yes.

C

Then, does it mean...

R. A. GOAL

Metatron, who visits you, is part of Jesus' space soul, right?

C
Yes, he is.

R. A. GOAL
Such space beings exist. There are space beings who carry out various tasks on other planets as well as on Earth. Some of them are here on Earth, taking on many tasks. We are engaged in such a mission.

I am one of the beings that represent the space soul of Shakyamuni Buddha, so I am connected to El Cantare. El Cantare and I are... well, my name is not listed as one of the brother souls of El Cantare in your books, but if you ask me about the network of El Cantare's space souls, I can say I am included.

Such knowledge will be revealed way out in the future, so I don't know how much I can reveal at this moment. You should live long.

C
I understand. This is such shocking news...

R. A. GOAL
Live long, and I will tell you everything.

C
Yes. I will continue to make effort.

R. A. GOAL
We want more power, more Light, and more believers. I want you to destroy the "wall" that blocks your way. It seems to us that something like the Berlin Wall is hindering your way. There is a kind of Berlin Wall in Japan, so you must destroy it. Beyond the wall is the land of freedom, so what are you waiting for? That is how we see things.

The voice of God is coming down to Japan

C
Master Ryuho Okawa published *The Laws of Secret* as the 2021 Laws Series, which is now spreading throughout the world. Master has given us precious teachings on the spiritual secrets of human existence. I'd like your advice on how we can strongly fulfill our mission this year to spread the truth that humans are essentially spiritual beings and have infinite power.

R. A. GOAL

All I can say is, you need to develop further. In fact, the reason why the teachings have yet to spread enough is because you lack faith. You don't really believe in those teachings. You haven't been able to believe the teachings truly from your heart because you think so many bizarre things are coming out.

Many people do business with China, travel there for business or sightseeing, or love Chinese food, so even if they read about the wrongdoings of China, they simply think our remarks are too harsh. Even if they hear about beings from space, they say such stories have been told from long ago and don't take them seriously. Some even think Earth is more advanced because humans have gone to outer space on a space shuttle.

Well, it's a pity. Earth's level is not high enough. The awareness of the earthlings is not high enough. It's too bad.

When there is information on the universe, the earthlings try to hide it and file it under the "X-files." Now that the U.S. president has been replaced... If Mr. Trump remained in office, he would have disclosed more information about the universe in an obvious manner, but I'm not sure how much information the Biden administration will disclose. Well, he may disclose some, but it's a bit of a shame. I'm afraid his level of awareness is not high enough. His level of awareness is extremely low.

Mr. Biden himself is said to be from the fifth dimensional Goodness Realm in the spirit world (see *Inside the Mind of President Biden*). If you ask me what level that is, I would say... well, he is not a bad person, but he is like a good-hearted chairperson of a neighborhood board, to be blunt. The fifth dimension is inhabited by such people. They are not bad people, and they have the ability to manage small neighborhood boards. Or, they can serve as a good-hearted police chief who does not take bribes. So, it's a pity that the U.S. is not making good use of its presidential position.

Mr. Trump called the media fake news because he probably had the ability to recognize the media's lies. So, it's a shame. This is truly regrettable. It's a shame America can't hear the voice of God.

But it's also important for them to realize that they are unable to hear the voice of God. You need to tell them, "The voice of God is coming down to Japan, so take the messages from Japan more seriously and make them guides for the future."

Accept the secrets of the universe with an unbiased, open mind

R. A. GOAL

This may sound radical, but as long as this sounds radical, there is no future for you. If you can say, "This is not radical at all but a matter of course," then the next truth will be revealed, followed by the truth after that. But as long as what I say sounds radical to you, you won't be able to hear further truths. We can't teach them to you.

We are now entering the era of "the Laws of the Universe," and this will probably continue to the end. These Laws will most probably be the last teachings, and there is much more to them.

Well, it's so frustrating. Even with your intellectual ability, you have yet to reach the required level. It's too bad. It's too bad your staff members don't study as hard as you do. What's more, you don't speak any foreign languages. It's too bad.

C

I'm sorry.

R. A. GOAL
If you had the ability to edit books in a foreign language, the teachings could have spread much further. Don't you think?

C
I'll work harder. I apologize for my lack of effort.

R. A. GOAL
Even today, I asked someone from International Headquarters to come, but there was no one available because they haven't studied enough. Although there are people with skills who can translate English into Japanese or Japanese into English, there is no one cultured enough to be able to spread the teachings in English, right? It's a pity, but they have to study harder. There are fewer than one in a hundred people who have the necessary level of awareness even among the staff members of Happy Science.

If your level of awareness is not high enough, at least be more open-minded and accept the teachings with a clean slate. If you can accept what we say, then we can reveal the next truths. If you don't, we can't advance any further. We'll have to stop there.

People are probably proud of many things they've accomplished in this world, such as the studies they did in the past, their qualifications, their doctor's degree, or being billionaires, but we don't care about those things. It has nothing to do with us. We are not interested in interacting with such people, either.

We intend to reveal the secrets of the universe, so we would really like people to develop the capacity to accept those secrets. We are full of such wishes. So, it's a shame you are unable to reach that level because of the constant worldly or secular worries, and troubles within and outside the organization. I sincerely hope you will help people realize that the Laws taught by Ryuho Okawa are the "Laws of the Messiah."

Oh, the next Laws Series, next year's Laws Series is *The Laws of the Messiah*. Go with *The Laws of the Messiah*. Messiah. It is too early to release *The Laws of the Universe* because there are still many truths that have yet to be revealed. So, let's go with *The Laws of the Messiah*.

C

OK. I can barely contain my surprise by the series of shocking truths you've revealed just now.

Be confident that you are ahead of the times

B

The U.S. and the world are in much chaos.

R. A. GOAL

Yes, so you have to be the leaders. Go for it.

B

Yes. The mission of Japan and the mission of Happy Science have become even greater.

R. A. GOAL

You all should be more confident. Happy Science University (HSU) has already surpassed Harvard University and so have you. Yes, you're way ahead of others. You should be confident in the fact that you are ahead of the times.

B

Yes, we understand. Thank you very much for your valuable message today under the title, "R. A. Goal's Words for the Future." Thank you very much.

R. A. GOAL

We have high hopes for you. Good luck.

B

Yes, thank you very much.

7

Make More Effort to Unveil the "Complete Scriptures of the Universe"

RYUHO OKAWA

[*Claps twice.*] OK. I think his true nature is being revealed little by little, but a great deal of information is probably still waiting to come out. Like the Tripitaka of Buddhism, it's the "Complete Scriptures of the Universe." There must be plenty of teachings. But those who have no idea what they are about won't understand even if we tell them. It's way beyond their level of understanding. Regardless, I must teach what I must as much as possible.

The Laws of the Universe movie series in and of themselves are also scriptures. In a sense, they are modern scriptures.

I want Happy Science to grow further. I want to be able to officially say that Happy Science has 20 million believers. After 20 million, our membership must multiply geometrically, in a "virus-like way." We must reach 100 million.

Christianity is a large organization, but it no longer has power. The pope may seem to be supported by a billion believers in his negotiation with China, but the one billion Catholic believers aren't taking any action. Most of them are Catholic just because they happened to be born in Catholic countries or to Catholic families. In reality, there aren't many who would fight against China for the sake of the pope.

Happy Science, on the other hand, is now trying to increase the number of believers who will actually take action. We must definitely accomplish what must be done and aim for the goal we must reach, as we were told in today's messages. This is certainly beyond the range of activities carried out by religious leaders and saviors in the past. It's definitely beyond their level. So, I must move forward as long as I live.

In the end, perhaps I will bid you adieu and truly leave for outer space. I might disappear on a flying saucer. Well, I don't know what would happen [*laughs*].

But while I'm on Earth, as much as possible... Unless you absorb my teachings and seek for more, they won't come out further. I think this is just the beginning. It's truly just the beginning, so it's sad. I want you to develop yourselves to another level.

B

Yes. We all need to make greater efforts.

RYUHO OKAWA

You should be more resilient against worldly setbacks.

B

I understand. Thank you very much for your valuable guidance.

RYUHO OKAWA

I'm counting on you.

Afterword

The Light penetrates the darkness of the universe and surely makes its way here.

It teaches us that the last Messiah has come.

To believe or not to believe—it will determine the future of humanity.

Will the world lose half its people through great disasters? Or will humanity overcome the wrong views of materialism, science, medicine, and communism, and open the way to a new world based on Truth, Goodness, and Beauty?

Humanity is now being tested. Fight through and win this battle, and you can open the Golden Age.

Ryuho Okawa
Master & CEO of Happy Science Group
February 23, 2021

ABOUT THE AUTHOR

RYUHO OKAWA was born on July 7th 1956, in Tokushima, Japan. After graduating from the University of Tokyo with a law degree, he joined a Tokyo-based trading house. While working at its New York headquarters, he studied international finance at the Graduate Center of the City University of New York. In 1981, he attained Great Enlightenment and became aware that he is El Cantare with a mission to bring salvation to all humankind. In 1986, he established Happy Science. It now has members in over 160 countries across the world, with more than 700 local branches and temples as well as 10,000 missionary houses around the world. The total number of lectures has exceeded 3,300 (of which more than 150 are in English) and over 2,850 books (of which more than 550 are Spiritual Interview Series) have been published, many of which are translated into 31 languages. Many of the books, including *The Laws of the Sun* have become best sellers or million sellers. To date, Happy Science has produced 23 movies. The original story and original concept were given by the Executive Producer Ryuho Okawa. Recent movie titles are *Beautiful Lure–A Modern Tale of "Painted Skin"* (live-action, May 2021), *Into the Dreams... and Horror Experiences* (live-action movie scheduled to be released in August 2021), and *The Laws of the Universe–The Age of Elohim* (animation movie scheduled to be released in Fall of 2021). He has also composed the lyrics and music of over 450 songs, such as theme songs and featured songs of movies. Moreover, he is the Founder of Happy Science University and Happy Science Academy (Junior and Senior High School), Founder and President of the Happiness Realization Party, Founder and Honorary Headmaster of Happy Science Institute of Government and Management, Founder of IRH Press Co., Ltd., and the Chairperson of NEW STAR PRODUCTION Co., Ltd. and ARI Production Co., Ltd.

WHAT IS EL CANTARE?

El Cantare means "the Light of the Earth," and is the Supreme God of the Earth who has been guiding humankind since the beginning of Genesis. He is whom Jesus called Father and Muhammad called Allah, and is the Creator in Shintoism, *Ame-no-Mioya-Gami*. Different parts of El Cantare's core consciousness have descended to Earth in the past, once as Alpha and another as Elohim. His branch spirits, such as Shakyamuni Buddha and Hermes, have descended to Earth many times and helped to flourish many civilizations. To unite various religions and to integrate various fields of study in order to build a new civilization on Earth, a part of the core consciousness has descended to Earth as Master Ryuho Okawa.

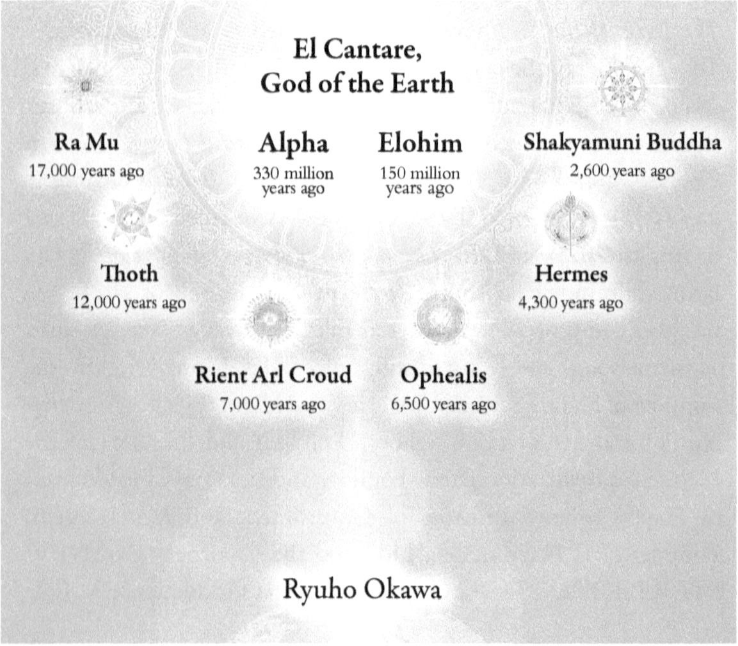

Alpha is a part of the core consciousness of El Cantare who descended to Earth around 330 million years ago. Alpha preached Earth's Truths to harmonize and unify Earth-born humans and space people who came from other planets.

Elohim is a part of El Cantare's core consciousness who descended to Earth around 150 million years ago. He gave wisdom, mainly on the differences of light and darkness, good and evil.

Shakyamuni Buddha was born as a prince into the Shakya Clan in India around 2,600 years ago. When he was 29 years old, he renounced the world and sought enlightenment. He later attained Great Enlightenment and founded Buddhism.

Hermes is one of the 12 Olympian gods in Greek mythology, but the spiritual Truth is that he taught the teachings of love and progress around 4,300 years ago that became the origin of the current Western civilization. He is a hero that truly existed.

Ophealis was born in Greece around 6,500 years ago and was the leader who took an expedition to as far as Egypt. He is the God of miracles, prosperity, and arts, and is known as Osiris in the Egyptian mythology.

Rient Arl Croud was born as a king of the ancient Incan Empire around 7,000 years ago and taught about the mysteries of the mind. In the heavenly world, he is responsible for the interactions that take place between various planets.

Thoth was an almighty leader who built the golden age of the Atlantic civilization around 12,000 years ago. In the Egyptian mythology, he is known as god Thoth.

Ra Mu was a leader who built the golden age of the civilization of Mu around 17,000 years ago. As a religious leader and a politician, he ruled by uniting religion and politics.

WHAT IS A SPIRITUAL MESSAGE?

We are all spiritual beings living on this earth. The following is the mechanism behind Master Ryuho Okawa's spiritual messages.

1 You are a spirit

People are born into this world to gain wisdom through various experiences and return to the other world when their lives end. We are all spirits and repeat this cycle in order to refine our souls.

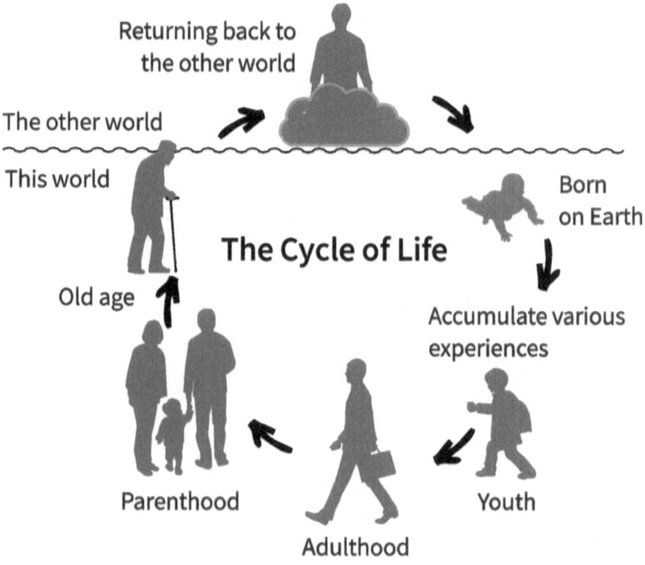

2 You have a guardian spirit

Guardian spirits are those who protect the people who are living on this earth. Each of us has a guardian spirit that watches over us and guides us from the other world. They were us in our past life, and are identical in how we think.

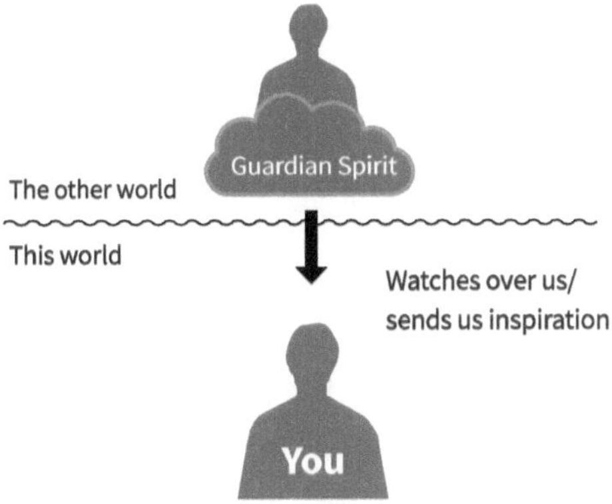

3 How spiritual messages work

Master Ryuho Okawa, through his enlightenment, is capable of summoning any spirit from anywhere in the world, including the spirit world.

Master Okawa's way of receiving spiritual messages is fundamentally different from that of other psychic mediums who undergo trances and are thereby completely taken over by the spirits they are channeling.

Master Okawa's attainment of a high level of enlightenment enables him to retain full control of his consciousness and body throughout the duration of the spiritual message. To allow the spirits to express their own thoughts and personalities freely, however, Master Okawa usually softens the dominancy of his consciousness. This way, he is able to keep his own philosophies out of the way and ensure that the spiritual messages are pure expressions of the spirits he is channeling.

Since guardian spirits think at the same subconscious level as the person living on earth, Master Okawa can summon the spirit and find out what the person on earth is actually thinking. If the person has already returned to the other world, the spirit can give messages to the people living on earth through Master Okawa.

Since 2009, more than 1,150 sessions of spiritual messages have been openly recorded by Master Okawa, and the majority of these have been published. Spiritual messages from the guardian spirits of people living today such as Donald Trump, former Japanese Prime Minister Shinzo Abe and Chinese President Xi Jinping, as well as spiritual messages sent from the spirit world by Jesus Christ, Muhammad, Thomas Edison, Mother Teresa, Steve Jobs and Nelson Mandela are just a tiny pack of spiritual messages that were published so far.

Domestically, in Japan, these spiritual messages are being read by a wide range of politicians and mass media, and the high-level contents of these books are delivering an impact even more on politics, news and public opinion. In recent years, there have been spiritual messages recorded in English, and English translations are being done on the spiritual messages given in Japanese. These have been published overseas, one after another, and have started to shake the world.

...
1 The guardian spirit / spirit in the other world...
2 Goes inside Master Okawa in this world
...
3 Master Okawa speaks the words of the guardian spirit / spirit

*For more about spiritual messages and a complete list of books in the Spiritual Interview Series, visit **okawabooks.com***

ABOUT HAPPY SCIENCE

Happy Science is a global movement that empowers individuals to find purpose and spiritual happiness and to share that happiness with their families, societies, and the world. With more than 12 million members around the world, Happy Science aims to increase awareness of spiritual truths and expand our capacity for love, compassion, and joy so that together we can create the kind of world we all wish to live in.

Activities at Happy Science are based on the Principles of Happiness (Love, Wisdom, Self-Reflection, and Progress). These principles embrace worldwide philosophies and beliefs, transcending boundaries of culture and religions.

Love teaches us to give ourselves freely without expecting anything in return; it encompasses giving, nurturing, and forgiving.

Wisdom leads us to the insights of spiritual truths, and opens us to the true meaning of life and the will of God (the universe, the highest power, Buddha).

Self-Reflection brings a mindful, nonjudgmental lens to our thoughts and actions to help us find our truest selves—the essence of our souls—and deepen our connection to the highest power. It helps us attain a clean and peaceful mind and leads us to the right life path.

Progress emphasizes the positive, dynamic aspects of our spiritual growth—actions we can take to manifest and spread happiness around the world. It's a path that not only expands our soul growth, but also furthers the collective potential of the world we live in.

PROGRAMS AND EVENTS

The doors of Happy Science are open to all. We offer a variety of programs and events, including self-exploration and self-growth programs, spiritual seminars, meditation and contemplation sessions, study groups, and book events.

Our programs are designed to:

* Deepen your understanding of your purpose and meaning in life
* Improve your relationships and increase your capacity to love unconditionally
* Attain peace of mind, decrease anxiety and stress, and feel positive
* Gain deeper insights and a broader perspective on the world
* Learn how to overcome life's challenges

... and much more.

For more information, visit ***happy-science.org****.*

OUR ACTIVITIES

Happy Science does other various activities to provide support for those in need.

- **You Are An Angel! General Incorporated Association**

  Happy Science has a volunteer network in Japan that encourages and supports children with disabilities as well as their parents and guardians.

- **Never Mind School for Truancy**

  At 'Never Mind,' we support students who find it very challenging to attend schools in Japan. We also nurture their self-help spirit and power to rebound against obstacles in life based on Master Okawa's teachings and faith.

- **"Prevention Against Suicide" Campaign since 2003**

  A nationwide campaign to reduce suicides; over 20,000 people commit suicide every year in Japan. "The Suicide Prevention Website-Words of Truth for You-" presents spiritual prescriptions for worries such as depression, lost love, extramarital affairs, bullying and work-related problems, thereby saving many lives.

- **Support for Anti-bullying Campaigns**

  Happy Science provides support for a group of parents and guardians, Network to Protect Children from Bullying, a general incorporated foundation launched in Japan to end bullying, including those that can even be called a criminal offense. So far, the network received more than 5,000 cases and resolved 90% of them.

- **The Golden Age Scholarship**

  This scholarship is granted to students who can contribute greatly and bring a hopeful future to the world.

- **Success No.1**
  Buddha's Truth Afterschool Academy

  Happy Science has over 180 classrooms throughout Japan and in several cities around the world that focus on afterschool education for children. The education focuses on faith and morals in addition to supporting children's school studies.

- **Angel Plan V**

  For children under the age of kindergarten, Happy Science holds classes for nurturing healthy, positive, and creative boys and girls.

- **Future Stars Training Department**

  The Future Stars Training Department was founded within the Happy Science Media Division with the goal of nurturing talented individuals to become successful in the performing arts and entertainment industry.

- **NEW STAR PRODUCTION Co., Ltd.**
  ARI Production Co., Ltd.

  We have companies to nurture actors and actresses, artists, and vocalists. They are also involved in film production.

ABOUT HAPPINESS REALIZATION PARTY

The Happiness Realization Party (HRP) was founded in May 2009 by Master Ryuho Okawa as part of the Happy Science Group to offer concrete and proactive solutions to the current issues such as military threats from North Korea and China and the long-term economic recession. HRP aims to implement drastic reforms of the Japanese government, thereby bringing peace and prosperity to Japan. To accomplish this, HRP proposes two key policies:

1) Strengthening the national security and the Japan-U.S. alliance, which plays a vital role in the stability of Asia.

2) Improving the Japanese economy by implementing drastic tax cuts, taking monetary easing measures and creating new major industries.

HRP advocates that Japan should offer a model of a religious nation that allows diverse values and beliefs to coexist, and that contributes to global peace.

For more information, visit ***en.hr-party.jp***

HAPPY SCIENCE ACADEMY JUNIOR AND SENIOR HIGH SCHOOL

Happy Science Academy Junior and Senior High School is a boarding school founded with the goal of educating the future leaders of the world who can have a big vision, persevere, and take on new challenges.

Currently, there are two campuses in Japan; the Nasu Main Campus in Tochigi Prefecture, founded in 2010, and the Kansai Campus in Shiga Prefecture, founded in 2013.

HAPPY SCIENCE UNIVERSITY

THE FOUNDING SPIRIT AND THE GOAL OF EDUCATION

Based on the founding philosophy of the university, "Exploration of happiness and the creation of a new civilization," education, research and studies will be provided to help students acquire deep understanding grounded in religious belief and advanced expertise with the objectives of producing "great talents of virtue" who can contribute in a broad-ranging way to serve Japan and the international society.

FACULTIES

Faculty of human happiness

Students in this faculty will pursue liberal arts from various perspectives with a multidisciplinary approach, explore and envision an ideal state of human beings and society.

Faculty of successful management

This faculty aims to realize successful management that helps organizations to create value and wealth for society and to contribute to the happiness and the development of management and employees as well as society as a whole.

Faculty of future creation

Students in this faculty study subjects such as political science, journalism, performing arts and artistic expression, and explore and present new political and cultural models based on truth, goodness and beauty.

Faculty of future industry

This faculty aims to nurture engineers who can resolve various issues facing modern civilization from a technological standpoint and contribute to the creation of new industries of the future.

CONTACT INFORMATION

Happy Science is a worldwide organization with faith centers around the globe. For a comprehensive list of centers, visit the worldwide directory at ***happy-science.org***. The following are some of the many Happy Science locations:

UNITED STATES AND CANADA

New York
79 Franklin St., New York, NY 10013
Phone: 212-343-7972
Fax: 212-343-7973
Email: ny@happy-science.org
Website: happyscience-usa.org

New Jersey
725 River Rd, #102B, Edgewater, NJ 07020
Phone: 201-313-0127
Fax: 201-313-0120
Email: nj@happy-science.org
Website: happyscience-usa.org

Florida
5208 8th St., Zephyrhills, FL 33542
Phone: 813-715-0000
Fax: 813-715-0010
Email: florida@happy-science.org
Website: happyscience-usa.org

Atlanta
1874 Piedmont Ave., NE Suite 360-C
Atlanta, GA 30324
Phone: 404-892-7770
Email: atlanta@happy-science.org
Website: happyscience-usa.org

San Francisco
525 Clinton St.
Redwood City, CA 94062
Phone & Fax: 650-363-2777
Email: sf@happy-science.org
Website: happyscience-usa.org

Los Angeles
1590 E. Del Mar Blvd., Pasadena, CA 91106
Phone: 626-395-7775
Fax: 626-395-7776
Email: la@happy-science.org
Website: happyscience-usa.org

Orange County
10231 Slater Ave., #204
Fountain Valley, CA 92708
Phone: 714-745-1140
Email: oc@happy-science.org
Website: happyscience-usa.org

San Diego
7841 Balboa Ave., Suite #202
San Diego, CA 92111
Phone: 626-395-7775
Fax: 626-395-7776
E-mail: sandiego@happy-science.org
Website: happyscience-usa.org

Hawaii
Phone: 808-591-9772
Fax: 808-591-9776
Email: hi@happy-science.org
Website: happyscience-usa.org

Kauai
3343 Kanakolu Street, Suite 5
Lihue, HI 96766, U.S.A.
Phone: 808-822-7007
Fax: 808-822-6007
Email: kauai-hi@happy-science.org
Website: happyscience-usa.org

Toronto
845 The Queensway
Etobicoke ON M8Z 1N6 Canada
Phone: 1-416-901-3747
Email: toronto@happy-science.org
Website: happy-science.ca

Vancouver
#201-2607 East 49th Avenue
Vancouver, BC, V5S 1J9, Canada
Phone: 1-604-437-7735
Fax: 1-604-437-7764
Email: vancouver@happy-science.org
Website: happy-science.ca

INTERNATIONAL

Tokyo
1-6-7 Togoshi, Shinagawa
Tokyo, 142-0041 Japan
Phone: 81-3-6384-5770
Fax: 81-3-6384-5776
Email: tokyo@happy-science.org
Website: happy-science.org

Seoul
74, Sadang-ro 27-gil,
Dongjak-gu, Seoul, Korea
Phone: 82-2-3478-8777
Fax: 82-2-3478-9777
Email: korea@happy-science.org
Website: happyscience-korea.org

London
3 Margaret St.
London,W1W 8RE United Kingdom
Phone: 44-20-7323-9255
Fax: 44-20-7323-9344
Email: eu@happy-science.org
Website: happyscience-uk.org

Taipei
No. 89, Lane 155, Dunhua N. Road
Songshan District, Taipei City 105, Taiwan
Phone: 886-2-2719-9377
Fax: 886-2-2719-5570
Email: taiwan@happy-science.org
Website: happyscience-tw.org

Sydney
516 Pacific Hwy, Lane Cove North,
NSW 2066, Australia
Phone: 61-2-9411-2877
Fax: 61-2-9411-2822
Email: sydney@happy-science.org

Malaysia
No 22A, Block 2, Jalil Link Jalan Jalil Jaya 2,
Bukit Jalil 57000, Kuala Lumpur, Malaysia
Phone: 60-3-8998-7877
Fax: 60-3-8998-7977
Email: malaysia@happy-science.org
Website: happyscience.org.my

Brazil Headquarters
Rua. Domingos de Morais 1154,
Vila Mariana, Sao Paulo SP
CEP 04009-002, Brazil
Phone: 55-11-5088-3800
Fax: 55-11-5088-3806
Email: sp@happy-science.org
Website: happyscience.com.br

Nepal
Kathmandu Metropolitan City Ward
No. 15,
Ring Road, Kimdol,
Sitapaila Kathmandu, Nepal
Phone: 97-714-272931
Email: nepal@happy-science.org

Jundiai
Rua Congo, 447, Jd. Bonfiglioli
Jundiai-CEP, 13207-340
Phone: 55-11-4587-5952
Email: jundiai@happy-science.org

Uganda
Plot 877 Rubaga Road, Kampala
P.O. Box 34130, Kampala, Uganda
Phone: 256-79-4682-121
Email: uganda@happy-science.org
Website: happyscience-uganda.org

ABOUT IRH PRESS

IRH Press Co., Ltd., based in Tokyo, was founded in 1987 as a publishing division of Happy Science. IRH Press publishes religious and spiritual books, journals, magazines and also operates broadcast and film production enterprises. For more information, visit *okawabooks.com*.

Follow us on:

Facebook: Okawa Books
Twitter: Okawa Books
Goodreads: Ryuho Okawa
Instagram: OkawaBooks
Pinterest: Okawa Books

NEWSLETTER

To receive book related news, promotions and events, please subscribe to our newsletter below.

https://okawabooks.us11.list-manage.com/subscribe?u=1fc70960eefd92668052ab7f8&id=2fbd8150ef

MEDIA

OKAWA BOOK CLUB

A conversation about Ryuho Okawa's titles, topics ranging from self-help, current affairs, spirituality and religions.

Available at iTunes, Spotify and Amazon Music.

Apple iTunes:
https://podcasts.apple.com/us/podcast/okawa-book-club/id1527893043

Spotify:
https://open.spotify.com/show/09mpgX2iJ6stVm4eBRdo2b

Amazon Music:
https://music.amazon.com/podcasts/7b759f24-ff72-4523-bfee-24f48294998f/Okawa-Book-Club

BOOKS BY RYUHO OKAWA

RYUHO OKAWA'S LAWS SERIES

The Laws Series is an annual volume of books that are mainly comprised of Ryuho Okawa's lectures on various topics that highlight principles and guidelines for the activities of Happy Science every year. *The Laws of the Sun*, the first publication of the laws series, ranked in the annual best-selling list in Japan in 1987. Since then, all of the laws series' titles have ranked in the annual best-selling list for more than two decades, setting socio-cultural trends in Japan and around the world.

The 27th Laws Series

THE LAWS OF SECRET

AWAKEN TO THIS NEW WORLD AND CHANGE YOUR LIFE

Paperback • 248 pages • $16.95
ISBN: 978-1-942125-81-5

Our physical world coexists with the multi-dimensional spirit world and we are constantly interacting with some kind of spiritual energy, whether positive or negative, without consciously realizing it. This book reveals how our lives are affected by invisible influences, including the spiritual reasons behind influenza, the novel coronavirus infection, and other illnesses.

The new view of the world in this book will inspire you to change your life in a better direction, and to become someone who can give hope and courage to others in this age of confusion.

For a complete list of books, visit ***okawabooks.com***

THE TRILOGY

The first three volumes of the Laws Series, *The Laws of the Sun*, *The Golden Laws*, and *The Nine Dimensions* make a trilogy that completes the basic framework of the teachings of God's Truths. *The Laws of the Sun* discusses the structure of God's Laws, *The Golden Laws* expounds on the doctrine of time, and *The Nine Dimensions* reveals the nature of space.

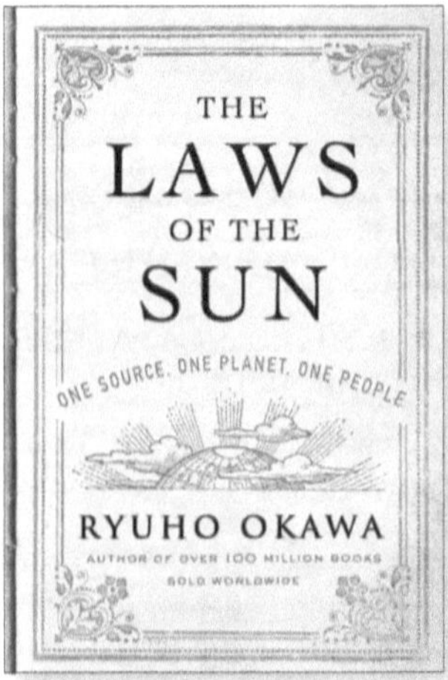

THE LAWS OF THE SUN

ONE SOURCE, ONE PLANET, ONE PEOPLE

Paperback • 288 pages • $15.95
ISBN: 978-1-942125-43-3

IMAGINE IF YOU COULD ASK GOD why He created this world and what spiritual laws He used to shape us—and everything around us. If we could understand His designs and intentions, we could discover what our goals in life should be and whether our actions move us closer to those goals or farther away.

At a young age, a spiritual calling prompted Ryuho Okawa to outline what he innately understood to be universal truths for all humankind. In *The Laws of the Sun*, Okawa outlines these laws of the universe and provides a road map for living one's life with greater purpose and meaning.

In this powerful book, Ryuho Okawa reveals the transcendent nature of consciousness and the secrets of our multidimensional universe and our place in it. By understanding the different stages of love and following the Buddhist Eightfold Path, he believes we can speed up our eternal process of development. *The Laws of the Sun* shows the way to realize true happiness—a happiness that continues from this world through the other.

For a complete list of books, visit ***okawabooks.com***

The Golden Laws

History through the Eyes of the Eternal Buddha

Paperback • 201 pages • $14.95

ISBN: 978-1-941779-81-1

Throughout history, Great Guiding Spirits of Light have been present on Earth in both the East and the West at crucial points in human history to further our spiritual development. *The Golden Laws* reveals how Divine Plan has been unfolding on Earth, and outlines 5,000 years of the secret history of humankind. Once we understand the true course of history, through past, present and into the future, we cannot help but become aware of the significance of our spiritual mission in the present age.

The Nine Dimensions

Unveiling the Laws of Eternity

Paperback • 168 pages • $15.95

ISBN: 978-0-982698-56-3

This book is a window into the mind of our loving God, who designed this world and the vast, wondrous world of our afterlife as a school with many levels through which our souls learn and grow. When the religions and cultures of the world discover the truth of their common spiritual origin, they will be inspired to accept their differences, come together under faith in God, and build an era of harmony and peaceful progress on Earth.

LAWS SERIES

THE LAWS OF HAPPINESS

LOVE, WISDOM, SELF-REFLECTION AND PROGRESS

Paperback • 264 pages • $16.95
ISBN: 978-1-942125-70-9

This book endeavors to answer the question, "What is true happiness?" This milestone text introduces four distinct principles, based on the "Laws of Mind" and sourced from Okawa's real-world experience, to guide readers towards sustainable happiness. Okawa's four "Principles of Happiness" present an easy, yet profound framework to ground this rapidly advanced and highly competitive society. In practice, Okawa outlines pragmatic steps to revitalize our ambition to lead a happier and meaningful life.

THE LAWS OF GREAT ENLIGHTENMENT

ALWAYS WALK WITH BUDDHA

Paperback • 232 pages • $17.95
ISBN: 978-1-942125-62-4

Constant self-blame for mistakes, setbacks, or failures and feelings of unforgivingness toward others are hard to overcome. Through the power of enlightenment we can learn to forgive ourselves and others, overcome life's problems, and courageously create a brighter future ourselves. *The Laws of Great Enlightenment* addresses the core problems of life that people often struggle with and offers advice on how to overcome them based on spiritual truths.

For a complete list of books, visit ***okawabooks.com***

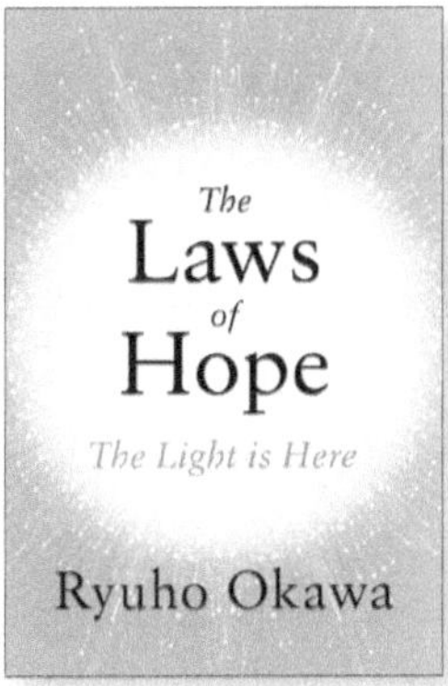

THE LAWS OF HOPE

THE LIGHT IS HERE

Paperback • 224 pages • $16.95

ISBN:978-1-942125-76-1

This book provides ways to bring light and hope to ourselves through our own efforts, even in the midst of sufferings and adversities. Inspired by a wish to bring happiness, success, and hope to humanity, Okawa shows us how to look at and think about our lives and circumstances. He says that hopes come true when we have the right mindset inside us.

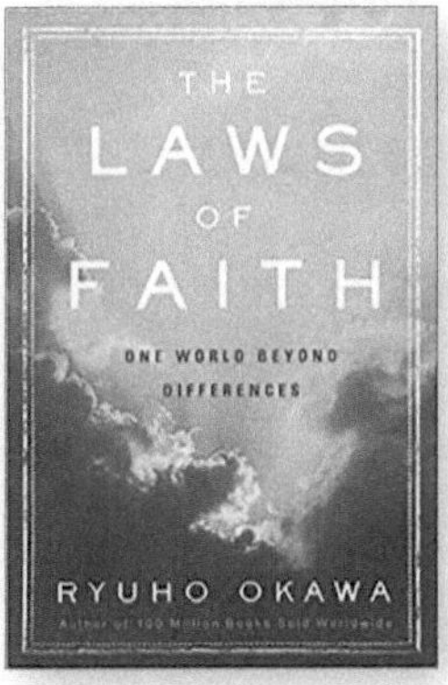

THE LAWS OF FAITH

ONE WORLD BEYOND DIFFERENCES

Paperback • 208 pages • $15.95

ISBN: 978-1-942125-34-1

Ryuho Okawa preaches at the core of a new universal religion from various angles while integrating logical and spiritual viewpoints in mind with current world situations. This book offers us the key to accept diversities beyond differences in ethnicity, religion, race, gender, descent, and so on, harmonize the individuals and nations and create a world filled with peace and prosperity.

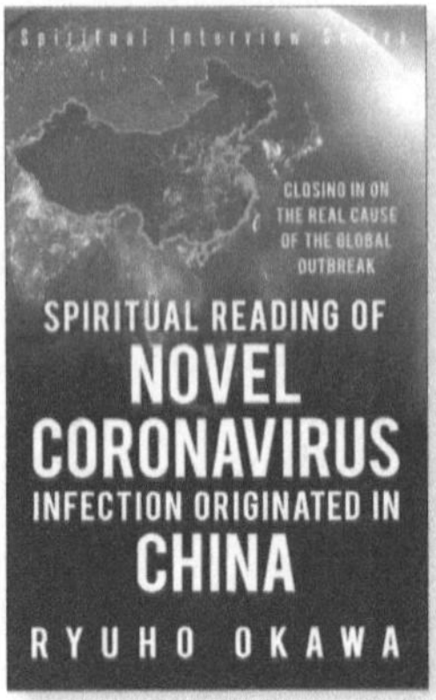

Spiritual Reading of Novel Coronavirus Infection Originated in China

Closing in on the Real Cause of the Global Outbreak

Paperback • 278 pages • $13.95
ISBN: 978-1-943869-77-0

This worldwide pandemic is not a mere act of nature nor a coincidence, but rather, heaven's warning to humanity, especially China. Through this book, you can find out "the immunity" against the novel coronavirus, among other shocking truths.

The Novel Coronavirus Originated in China: Lessons for Humankind

Spiritual Messages from Shibasaburo Kitasato and R. A. Goal

Paperback • 228 pages • $13.95
ISBN: 978-1-943869-88-6

This book records spiritual messages from a bacteriologist and a space being. They disclose many truths about the novel coronavirus pandemic, such as China's hidden secrets, what the future holds, and hopeful messages for humanity. Only when humanity learns what we are to learn from this pandemic, can we escape this worldwide crisis and create a new age.

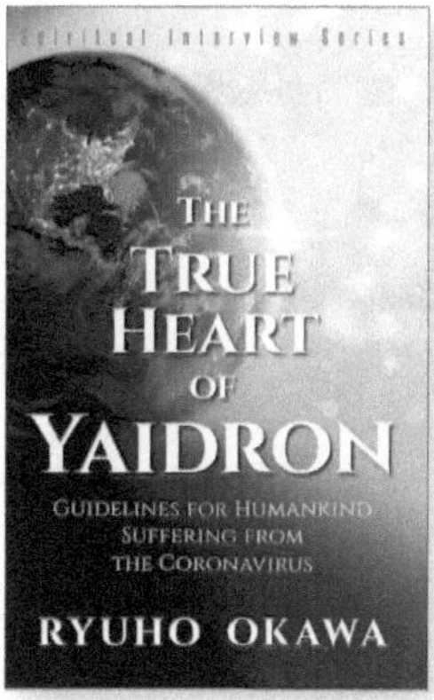

The True Heart of Yaidron

Guidelines for Humankind Suffering from the Coronavirus

Paperback • 144 pages • $11.95
ISBN: 978-1-943928-04-0

What are the real cause and evil schemes behind the worldwide coronavirus crisis? Out of compassion, this book reveals truths about the all-out global war now being waged by the evil power in East Asia that's destroying the power of the people. Discover the movement that's trying to bring together the powers of the West, India, and Asia by the belief of "With Savior," to save humankind and create the new golden future of Earth.

With Savior

Messages from Space Being Yaidron

Paperback • 232 pages • $13.95
ISBN: 978-1-943869-94-7

The human race is now faced with multiple unprecedented crises. Perhaps God is warning us humans to reconsider our materialistic and arrogant ways. Fortunately, God has sent us a savior, who is now teaching us to repent and showing us the path we should choose. In this book, space being Yaidron sends his warnings and messages of hope.

CONSIDERING THE FUTURE OF THE WORLD

TRUMP SHALL NEVER DIE

HIS DETERMINATION TO COME BACK

Paperback • 206 pages • $11.95
ISBN: 978-1-943928-08-8

This book unveiled Mr. Donald Trump's true thoughts never reported by the media through spiritual interview with the guardian spirit of him. The topics include the "madness" found in GAFA and the mainstream media, Mr. Trump's views on the coronavirus vaccine and global warming, and the true aim of "Make America Great Again."

THE XI JINPING THOUGHT NOW

Paperback • 212 pages • $13.95
ISBN: 978-1-943928-05-7

With the launch of Biden administration in the U.S. and the 100th anniversary of the founding of the Chinese Communist Party approaching, China has been expanding its military threat and reinforcing its influence over the world. What urges China to seek global hegemony? This book unveils the "dark being" behind the Xi Jinping Thought.

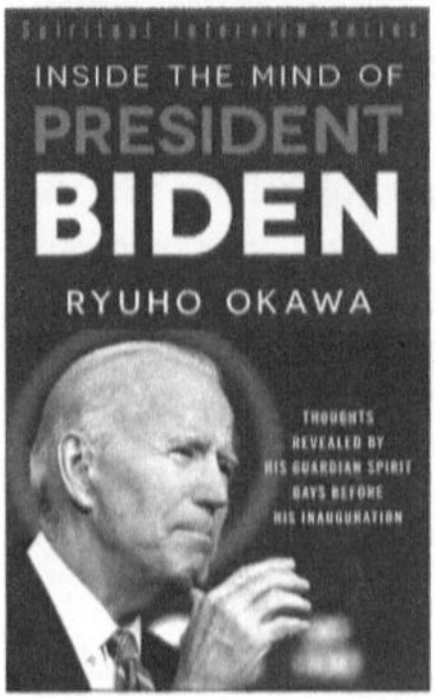

INSIDE THE MIND OF PRESIDENT BIDEN

THOUGHTS REVEALED BY HIS GUARDIAN SPIRIT DAYS BEFORE HIS INAUGURATION

Paperback • 296 pages • $13.95
ISBN: 978-1-943928-02-6

What are the real thoughts inside the mind of President Biden? What scheme does he know about the coronavirus crisis and the Obama administration's close ties with Beijing? You'll discover whether he can truly fulfill the responsibilities of an American president and a major world leader and also about the way he views the battle between democracy and totalitarianism we are now witnessing.

*For a complete list of books, visit **okawabooks.com***

BOOKS ON SURVIVING IN THE AGE OF CRISIS

HOW TO SURVIVE THE CORONAVIRUS RECESSION

Paperback • 171 pages • $14.95
ISBN: 978-1-943869-97-8

From the perspectives of both economics and health, this book delves into how you can survive the coronavirus recession. As taught by the author Ryuho Okawa, there is a strong relationship between your spiritual health and immunity, and he demonstrates the mindset you should have as well as introduces a very effective meditation that you can do to truly strengthen your immunity.

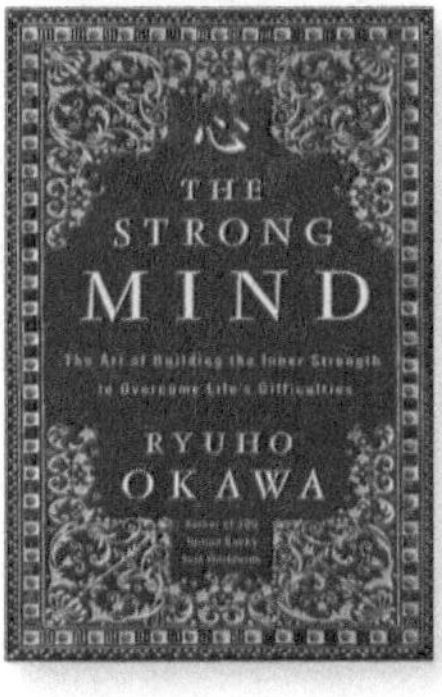

THE STRONG MIND

THE ART OF BUILDING THE INNER STRENGTH TO OVERCOME LIFE'S DIFFICULTIES

Paperback • 192 pages • $15.95
ISBN: 978-1-942125-36-5

The strong mind is what we need to rise time and again, and to move forward no matter what difficulties we face in life. This book will inspire and empower you to take courage, develop a mature and cultivated heart, and achieve resilience and hardiness so that you can break through the barriers of your limits and keep winning in the battle of your life.

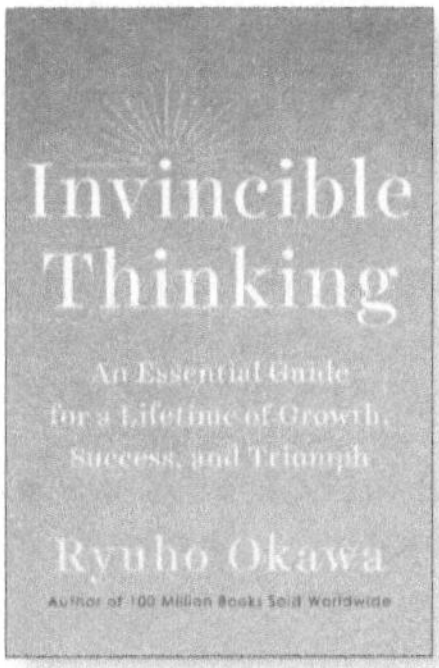

INVINCIBLE THINKING

AN ESSENTIAL GUIDE FOR A LIFETIME OF GROWTH, SUCCESS, AND TRIUMPH

Hardcover • 208 pages • $16.95
ISBN: 978-1-942125-25-9

In this book, Ryuho Okawa lays out the principles of invincible thinking that will allow us to achieve long-lasting triumph. This powerful and unique philosophy is not only about becoming successful or achieving our goal in life, but also about building the foundation of life that becomes the basis of our life-long, lasting success and happiness.

For a complete list of books, visit ***okawabooks.com***

BOOKS ON THE TRUTH OF THE SPIRIT WORLD

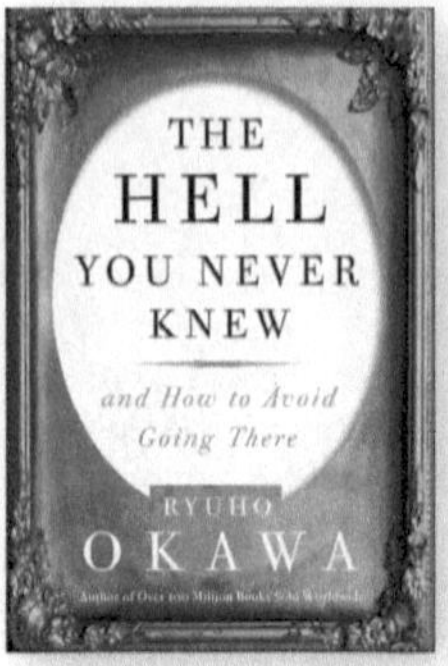

THE HELL YOU NEVER KNEW

AND HOW TO AVOID GOING THERE

Paperback • 192 pages • $15.95
ISBN: 978-1-942125-52-5

From ancient times, people have been warned of the danger of falling to Hell. But does the world of Hell truly exist? If it does, what kind of people would go there? Through his spiritual abilities, Ryuho Okawa found out that Hell is only a small part of the vast Spirit World, yet more than half of the people today go there after they die.

THE REAL EXORCIST

ATTAIN WISDOM TO CONQUER EVIL

Paperback • 208 pages • $16.95
ISBN:978-1-942125-67-9

This is a profound spiritual text backed by the author's nearly 40 years of real-life experience with spiritual phenomena. In it, Okawa teaches how we may discern and overcome our negative tendencies, by acquiring the right knowledge, mindset and lifestyle.

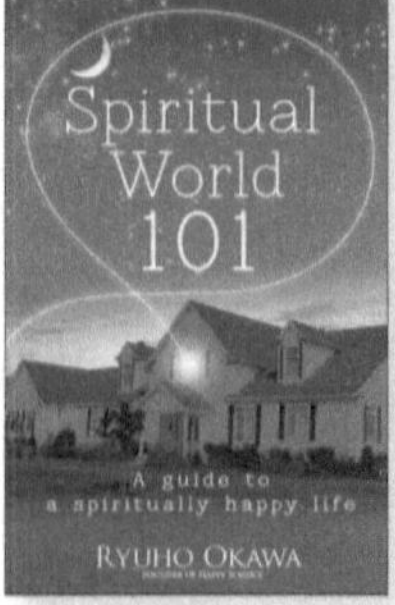

SPIRITUAL WORLD 101

A GUIDE TO A SPIRITUALLY HAPPY LIFE

Paperback • 184 pages • $14.95
ISBN: 978-1-941779-43-9

This book is a spiritual guidebook that will answer all your questions about the spiritual world, with illustrations and diagrams explaining about your guardian spirit and the secrets of God and Buddha. By reading this book, you will be able to understand the true meaning of life and find happiness in everyday life.

For a complete list of books, visit ***okawabooks.com***

THE TRUE EIGHTFOLD PATH

GUIDEPOSTS FOR SELF-INNOVATION

Paperback • 272 pages • $16.95
ISBN: 978-1-942125-80-8

This book explains how we can apply the Eightfold Path, one of the main pillars of Shakyamuni Buddha's teachings, as everyday guideposts in the modern-age to achieve self-innovation to live better and make positive changes in these uncertain times.

THE ESSENCE OF BUDDHA

THE PATH TO ENLIGHTENMENT

Paperback • 208 pages • $14.95
ISBN: 978-1-942125-06-8

In this book, Ryuho Okawa imparts in simple and accessible language his wisdom about the essence of Shakyamuni Buddha's philosophy of life and enlightenment–teachings that have been inspiring people all over the world for over 2,500 years. By offering a new perspective on core Buddhist thoughts, Okawa brings these teachings to life for modern people. This book distills a way of life that anyone can practice to achieve a life of self-growth, compassionate living, and true happiness.

THE MIRACLE OF MEDITATION

OPENING YOUR LIFE TO PEACE, JOY, AND THE POWER WITHIN

Paperback • 207 pages • $15.95
ISBN: 978-1-942125-09-9

This book introduces various types of meditation, including calming meditation, purposeful meditation, reading meditation, reflective meditation, and meditation to communicate with heaven. Through reading and practicing meditation in this book, we can experience the miracle of meditation, which is to start living a life of peace, happiness, and success.

For a complete list of books, visit ***okawabooks.com***

UFOS CAUGHT ON CAMERA!
A Spiritual Investigation on Videos and Photos of the Luminous Objects Visiting Earth

THE LAWS OF SUCCESS
A Spiritual Guide to Turning Your Hopes into Reality

THE STARTING POINT OF HAPPINESS
An Inspiring Guide to Positive Living with Faith, Love, and Courage

WORRY-FREE LIVING
Let Go of Stress and Live in Peace and Happiness

THE MIRACLE OF MEDITATION
Opening Your Life to Peace, Joy, and the Power Within

THE TRUE EIGHTFOLD PATH
Guideposts for Self-innovation

THINK BIG!
Be Positive and Be Brave to Achieve Your Dreams

CHANGE YOUR LIFE, CHANGE THE WORLD
A Spiritual Guide to Living Now

INVITATION TO HAPPINESS
7 Inspirations from Your Inner Angel

For a complete list of books, visit ***okawabooks.com***

MUSIC BY RYUHO OKAWA

THE THUNDER

a composition for repelling the Coronavirus

We have been granted this music from our Lord. It will repel away the novel Coronavirus originated in China. Experience this magnificent powerful music.

Search on YouTube

the thunder coronavirus for a short ad!

THE EXORCISM

prayer music for repelling Lost Spirits

Feel the divine vibrations of this Japanese and Western exorcising symphony to banish all evil possessions you suffer from and to purify your space!

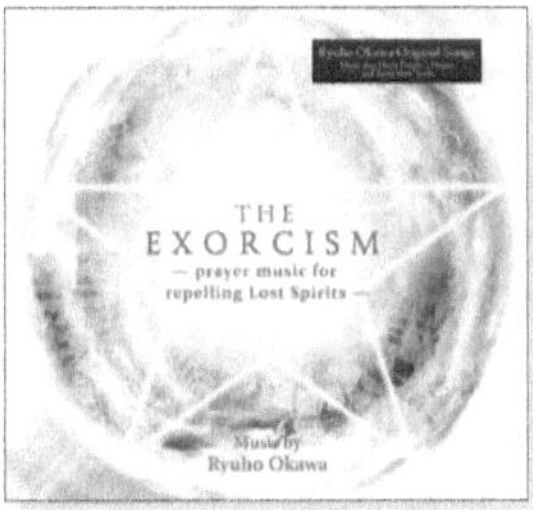

Search on YouTube

the exorcism repelling for a short ad!

Available online
Spotify iTunes Amazon

CD available at Happy Science local branches and shoja (temples)

www.ingramcontent.com/pod-product-compliance
Lightning Source LLC
Chambersburg PA
CBHW030152100526
44592CB00009B/232
9781943928101